NOTES

Eleanor Coppola

SIMON AND SCHUSTER • NEW YORK

Published by Simon and Schuster
A Division of Gulf & Western Corporation
Simon & Schuster Building
Rockefeller Center
1230 Avenue of the Americas
New York, New York 10020

Designed by Eve Metz
Manufactured in the United States of America

1 2 3 4 5 6 7 8 9 10

Library of Congress Cataloging in Publication Data

Coppola, Eleanor.
    Notes.
    1. Apocalypse now. [Motion picture] 2. Coppola,
Francis Ford, 1939–   I. Title.
PN1997.A653C6   791.43'7   79-11578

ISBN 0-671-24838-3

TO MY FAMILY

Acknowledgment

I started writing these notes for myself without intending that they be read by anyone else, but then I sent a few pages in letters to friends while I was in the Philippines. I want to thank Arlene Bernstein, Marti Sternberg and my mother for saying "Send more." This kept me writing when I might have drifted to a stop. Last year my husband read all my notes. He recognized they could be a book and encouraged me to publish them. I thank him. I appreciate Fred Roos's casting me with the perfect editor, Nan Talese, whose vision, taste and attention to every detail gave the book its form and shaped the content.

Contents

Prologue

Telephone Calls—November 1975 to February 1976

Steve McQueen says the script is great, but the part of Willard is not really right for him. Francis says he will come down to Malibu and talk about rewriting the part for him.

Ten Days Later

Steve McQueen says he feels much better about the part, it is really a good script, but he can't really leave the country for seventeen weeks because Ali can't take her son out of the country and his son is graduating from high school.

The Next Day

Francis calls Brando. He doesn't answer. Francis talks to Brando's agent who says that he is not interested in a part and doesn't want to talk about it.

The Same Day

Francis talks to Al Pacino, tells him he is sending him the script. Discusses an interesting new approach to the character.

Later

Al has read the script and talks for hours about the part of Willard, what a great script it is, how he sees the part, but concludes with the realization that he can't do it because he wouldn't be able to stand seventeen weeks in the jungle. They remember how sick Al got in a few weeks in the Dominican Republic during *Godfather Part II*.

Francis talks to McQueen's agent and offers him the part of Kurtz, which is only for three weeks.

McQueen's agent says that Steve will do it, but that he wants the same money as for the seventeen-week part, $3 million, because the film will earn it back in foreign sales anyway.

Francis calls Jimmy Caan. Offers him the part of Willard—seventeen weeks, at $1.25 million.

Jimmy's agent says that he wants $2 million.

Francis offers Jimmy's agent $1.25 million again.

Jimmy turns it down, also says his wife is pregnant and doesn't want to have her baby in the Philippines.

Francis offers the Willard part to Jack Nicholson's agent. The agent turns it down for Jack because the film Jack will direct conflicts.

Francis calls Redford and he has finally read the script and thinks it is great. He likes the Kurtz part, but can't consider the Willard part because his film is not finished and he has promised his family that he will not leave for a long location the rest of this year.

Francis cancels his offer to McQueen.

Francis calls Jack Nicholson's agent and offers him the Kurtz part.

Francis talks to a casting director to set up casting calls in New York for unknown actors for the Willard part.

Jack's agent calls back. Jack says no to the Kurtz part.

Francis is back from New York, having talked to Al about playing Kurtz, and rewriting the part for him. Al says the part isn't right for him yet. Francis says that he needs a commitment before he can continue writing because the production date is closing in. Al says he can't commit. Francis says, "Trust me, together we can make it great." Al finally says he can't commit.

Francis feels very frustrated. He gathers up his Oscars and throws them out the window. The children pick up the pieces in the backyard. Four of the five are broken.

Brando's agent calls Francis and says Brando wants to see him.

Francis sets up a casting call for unknown actors in Los Angeles.

Introduction

On March 1, 1976, I went to the Philippines with my husband, Francis Coppola, our three children, Gio, Roman and Sofia, Francis's nephew, Marc, our housekeeper, baby-sitter and Francis's projectionist. We rented a large house in Manila for all of us to live in during the five-month scheduled shooting of Francis's film *Apocalypse Now*, an adventure set in Vietnam.

The Philippines was chosen as the location because of the similarity of the terrain to Vietnam, the fact that the Philippine Government was willing to rent its American-made helicopters and military equipment to the production and that building and labor costs were generally low.

Francis financed the film in advance by preselling the distribution rights to foreign countries and to United Artists in the United States. He raised approximately $13 million. The film was budgeted at $12–$14 million. By financing the film in this way, Francis retained ownership and control of it, but also had financial responsibility if the film went over budget.

The film was conceived as an action/adventure. The script was structured on Joseph Conrad's novel *Heart of Darkness*, but rather than Africa in the 1800s, the film was set on a river in Vietnam during the late sixties. The original screenplay was written by John Milius in 1969. Francis began rewrites in the fall of 1975. The story concerns a Captain Willard who is given an assignment to go on a classified mission up a river in Vietnam, cross into Cambodia and assassinate Colonel Kurtz. Kurtz is a Green Beret colonel who has apparently gone insane and is conducting the war by his own rules from an old Cambodian temple. His troops are a small band of renegade American soldiers and a tribe of local Montagnard Indians he has trained and armed. The script deals with Willard's journey and the events along the way. When Willard finally arrives at his destination, he has been changed by the experience of making the journey. Many of the people who worked on the film were also changed.

PART ONE

1976

March 4, Baler

It was the first time any of us had seen water buffalo, rice paddies and nipa huts. We crossed over the bridge at the edge of the little village and entered the deep foliage. Sofia said, "It looks like the Disneyland Jungle Cruise." The road ended at the beach and our jeep continued along the sand with the ocean on one side and the jungle on the other. We arrived at a lagoon near the mouth of a river and got into a bonca that took us across to the location for Village II. Dean's crew had cleared jungle, brought logs down the river to build a bridge, taught the local workers how to make adobe bricks, carted bamboo from the next province, built houses, pumped water, planted vegetables—created a complete Vietnamese village. Pigs rooted beside the road, chickens scratched under the houses, baskets of rice were drying in the town square, curtains flapped at the windows, cooking pots were neatly stacked for the next meal. I could hear the wind in the tall palm trees, but layers of sound seemed to be missing. There were no people.

March 9, Manila

The family is here in this large house. It is open and spacious and very grand by local standards. It is in Dasmariñas, the Beverly Hills of Manila. I asked the set dresser to furnish it with wicker so that when the film is over I could take it home for our country house in the Napa Valley. He used peacock chairs and rattan with velvet. There are ceiling fans and lots of tropical plants. People are coming in for a production meeting at the huge dining table. A houseboy in a white jacket is asking each person if they would like calamanci juice or a slice of papaya. It looks like the lobby of the Luau Restaurant.

I can hear workmen hand-digging a swimming pool in the backyard. A carpenter is pounding on the new wall of the projection booth.

The last few days we traveled by jet, helicopter, jeep, canoe and on foot to see all the locations where the film will be shot. We passed thatched houses on stilts, fishermen in outrigger canoes, little kids riding water buffalo. We drank from fresh coconuts. There were banana and palm trees, patches of thick jungle, miles and miles of rice paddies, sugarcane fields, little villages with people smiling and waving. At one of the locations a crewman had just killed a cobra snake. I wonder what the children think. Sofia is four, Roman is ten, Gio is twelve. My reality feels like a foreign movie. Part of me is waiting for the reels to change and get back to a familiar scene in San Francisco or Napa.

March 11, Manila

I have just been at the production office. The company has rented a section of one of the Philippine film studios in downtown Manila. I passed by the art department. Dean Tavoularis, the production designer, was there and his brother Alex, Angelo Graham, Bob Nelson, and their construction chief, John La Sandra. I hadn't seen them all together since *Godfather II*. It felt like seeing cousins and uncles. There were offices with people poring over maps, interviewing pilots and truck drivers and planning how to get the company to the first major location, Baler, which is six hours away over rough dirt roads. It is thirty minutes by plane. They were planning where hundreds of people could be housed and fed. Baler is a little town with only one small hotel.

Downstairs was a room as big as a gymnasium, filled with rows and rows of costumes. Several busloads of young men were getting haircuts and being fitted with GI wardrobe. Outside was a large studio with a sculptor and five or six assistants carving the huge head and temple decorations in clay that will be cast for the temple buildings at the main set called Kurtz Compound. They were working from Dean's drawings and photographs of Angkor Wat. The model for the big head was a beautiful young Filipina maid from a nearby boardinghouse. Now she was sitting in the studio by the window in the afternoon light listening to the radio and crocheting. In the parking lot, truckloads of electrical equipment and camera gear were being checked over. Francis introduced me to his cinematographer, Vittorio Storaro. He looked like a northern Italian prince. He had light brown hair and a face like in those Renaissance paintings. We met his camera operator, Enrico; his key grip, Alfredo; Alfredo's son, Mauro, a camera assistant; his brother, Mario; the lighting gaffer, Luciano; and perhaps a dozen others, all of whom spoke no English. They seemed to be a kind of family. Vittorio said that they had worked with him on *The Conformist*, *Last Tango in Paris*, and *1900*. On the back of one of the trucks, two men were heating a little espresso pot over a can of Sterno. We stopped with them for an afternoon coffee. They showed us their stash of Italian olive oil, canned tomatoes and boxes of spaghetti neatly packed in the crate they were sitting on.

March 13, Manila

Six cases of camera and sound equipment have just been delivered inside the front door. Francis has asked me to make the documentary film for the United Artists publicity department. I don't know if he is just trying to keep me busy or if he wants to avoid the addition of a professional team on an already overloaded production. Maybe both. He said I could hire a cameraman and sound man and just tell them what to do. I have no idea how to begin. I've done some still photography. Once I made a three-minute film. But that's it.

March 20

It is the first day of shooting. There is a current of excitement. The location is a salt farm next to a river. The scene is the helicopter bringing Willard to meet the patrol boat that will take him on his mission. The assistant director is calling over the PA system to the boat traffic to take their positions for a rehearsal. A painter is still painting the dock. Francis and Dean and the wardrobe man are with Willard, trying to decide which hat he should wear. I was just invited inside a local house at the river's edge. The first floor was mud with several chickens wandering around. There was one gas burner, a place for a wood fire, a table, a blue plastic dishpan, a bucket of water and a shelf of assorted dishes and pots. I took my shoes off to go upstairs into the one eight-by-twelve-foot room. There was a wooden bench, a cupboard and a wooden-slatted low table, which I was told was the bed. There seemed to be about six or eight members of the family. The man spoke some English. He said he had a cousin who was a nurse in Maryland.

March 24, Manila

I am in Sofia's room, sitting in one of her miniature chairs. She is at the table drawing a picture of two palm trees with a family in between. Yesterday I ate lunch at a little road-

25

side stand. It must have been too native for me. I stayed home today to be close to the bathroom. I have the air conditioner up all the way. Francis doesn't seem to be bothered by the heat. I start to feel faint by the afternoon when I am outside all day.

Philippine mosquitoes don't seem to be put off by Cutter's insect repellent. Sofia is covered with bites.

April 2, Baler

The helicopters used in the film are from the Philippine Air Force. Today, in the middle of the rehearsal for a complicated shot, they were called away to fight the rebels in a civil war about 150 miles to the south.

It is hard to know what is going on. There is no news of the war in the government-controlled press. I was talking to one of the Filipino crewmen. He said that a group of southern islands, which are predominantly Moslem, are fighting for independence. Francis has a government-supplied bodyguard at all times. There are guards at our house. The government seems to feel that if Francis were kidnapped by rebels, they might create an incident that could attract international attention.

April 4, Manila

Gio has been sick for nearly three weeks. He has had a slight fever, a stomachache, a headache. The doctor has been here four times. Yesterday he said, "Mrs. Coppola, I think your son is homesick." This morning Gio had no fever. He got up and went to school.

April 8, Baler

There is a rumor that rebels are in the hills about ten miles away. The Philippine Air Force is afraid there could be an attack on the helicopters, so they've withdrawn them to a base in Manila. Francis is frustrated that he doesn't have the aircraft he had been promised and must figure out how to keep shooting by rescheduling around them.

Thirty security specialists have been brought in to guard the large supply of explosives which the special effects department has and the M-16 automatic rifles the extras use. There is that tension of knowing that an incident could close down the production.

April 8, Baler

Last night Francis had a birthday party on the beach across
from the set. About three hundred people were invited, the
cast, crew and the American and Vietnamese extras and
some townspeople. Hundreds of pounds of hamburger and
hot dogs were shipped from San Francisco. The band and
food were flown in from Manila. They arrived at the beach
in several trucks just as it was getting dark. The birthday
cake was six feet by eight feet. It was made of twelve sheet
cakes iced together. Two men decorated it in the light of
the bandstand. They made mountains, a river, an ocean
and waves of icing. They planted paper palm trees, little
cardboard huts and a bridge to look like the set. They
placed plastic helicopters, boats, soldiers, flags, flowers and
candles, and letters that spelled "Happy Birthday, Francis,
Apocalypse Now."

A thick smoke blew from the barbecues; someone had
forgotten the spatulas and people were trying to turn their
hamburgers with pieces of cardboard. A lot of meat fell
through the grills and burned on the coals. It was a warm
night. There were no more cold drinks. Some people said
not enough had been ordered. Others said guys were grab-
bing cases and running off down the beach in the dark.

A team of ladies with knives to serve the cake began
removing the decorations and cutting slices at the bottom,
while the decorators were still working on the top. I could
hear two GI extras talking. They were standing on a bench
behind me. One said, "Wow, this is the most decadence
I've ever seen."

April 9, Baler

Several hundred South Vietnamese people were recruited from a refugee camp near Manila to play North Vietnamese in the film. As I passed their rest area today they were rehearsing a little play while they waited for the next shot. They speak no English but one young man called out "Stand by," and everyone got quiet and ready. Then he clapped two sticks together and called "Action" and the play began in Vietnamese. Later I noticed the group leader calling lunch the same way. He said "Stand by" and they all assembled; he clapped his sticks and called "Action," and they walked to lunch in a neat line.

April, Baler

I finally figured out why the toilet seats in the outhouses have footprints on them. Some large American designed the base so high that no Vietnamese or Filipino could possibly sit on the seat and touch the floor. They must stand on the seats and squat.

April 10, Manila

I like our laundry maid Cecilia, but it really bothers me that I have a human washing machine. She washes everything in the laundry tub by hand and irons in this heat. She is also the dishwasher. It makes me feel bad when I put my dirty clothes in the basket. I was complaining to the woman next door. She told me that Cecilia was glad to have a job with a nice family, that I was providing much needed employment. She earns, in pesos, about $55 a month plus room and board. Here a major appliance costs more.

April 12, Baler

I am sitting on some sandbags in the schoolhouse waiting for the big shot . . . eight helicopters will come from the sea, blow up two houses and some palm trees . . . turn out, pass back over, hit two more houses, pass again and blow up four houses and the boats on the beach. Special effects men have already started fires in the huts at the perimeter. They are throwing rubber tires in the flames to keep the black smoke billowing up. The helicopters are refueling. A description of what's happening three miles away is coming over the radio. "The engines are now turning over. They are now airborne."

Later

The next thing we knew, the shot began. Extras ran in front of us, two houses blew up and the fire started. The smoke blew at us. I had to stop shooting. I moved the camera and tripod. As I tried to level the camera I turned the knob the wrong way and it fell off in my hand. I didn't get the second shot until the houses on the left side of the village square were already on fire. There was so much noise, I didn't hear my camera run out. I don't know how much I missed. I changed magazines finally, and got some more shots of the house burning by the bridge. The smoke was so thick my eyes burned, my nose ran and I couldn't see anything, so I stopped shooting. I heard a lot of shouting. The paint shop and the prop storage with the stunt men's equipment was burning. My supplies were in the same building. I ran over and saw my three camera cases melted in the doorway. The wind had blown the fire across the road. When the paint cans started to explode, the men with the fire hoses ran. People wandered in and out of the smoke for a long time, trying to find their equipment. The stunt men were the hardest hit. They'll have to go back to Los Angeles; their custom-made asbestos safety suits melted. There was $30,000 to $50,000 worth of damage. People thought I was crying because Francis was mad that I lost my camera gear. My eyes were running from all the smoke.

April, Baler

They put the helicopter doors on with safety pins through the hinges so they can take the doors off fast to mount the cameras.

April, Baler

I was thinking about time, how on a movie set the shot is maintained in the same time no matter how many takes and hours pass. Reflectors and lights are added, footprints are smoothed away, so there are no telltale clues as the day wears on. When the shot is finished and the plugs are pulled, time seems to leap forward in a matter of seconds. Perhaps making movies is a step toward being able to move backward and forward and in and out of linear time.

April 13, Baler

It is eight o'clock in the morning, and so incredibly hot. If just a little breeze would come up and move the humid, still air. Last night we stayed in Baler. There was only fried chicken to eat. There were no vegetables to buy in town and the plane didn't come in from Manila. We ate spaghetti with the Italian crew at their house. Their supply of canned tomatoes, olive oil and pasta they brought from Italy is dwindling. I hear they have ordered more to be sent with the next film shipment from Rome. They finally got the local bakery to make them some Italian-style bread without sugar and milk in it.

April 14, Manila

It will be Easter in a few days. Several weeks ago I asked the little boy next door where he got his U.S. Easter egg dye. He said he got it on the black market. After that I began to notice odd things that appear in the supermarket, like several cases of Best Foods mayonnaise cheaper than I buy it at home. Then it disappeared and I haven't seen any since.

April 16, Manila

Last night Francis saw the assembly of the first week's rushes. They were the scenes with Harvey Keitel, who plays Willard. Afterward he sat down on the couch with the editors and Gray and Fred, the producers. He said "Well, what do you think?" I went upstairs to say good night to the boys, and when I came down about fifteen minutes later, they were already on the phone making plane reservations for flights to L.A. The next day, Francis had made the decision to replace his leading man. Gray said, "Jesus, Francis, how do you have the guts to do it?"

This morning Francis got up even earlier than usual. He didn't sleep much during the night. He started shaving his beard off. When he got down to the breakfast table about 6:00 A.M., the boys were pretty surprised. He has been wearing contact lenses lately because it is easier to look through the camera without glasses, and he's lost about thirty-five pounds. He really did look different. He said he wanted to go to L.A. and not be noticed by the press. He didn't want a lot of rumors to start about the film being in trouble before he had a chance to recast the part. Later he said he shaved off his beard to prove to himself, as a sort of outward symbol, that even when he is really in trouble he is capable of change.

Sofia was still asleep when he left for shooting. She had never seen him without a beard in her life. I decided to take her to the airport this evening to meet the plane from Baler and see him off to L.A. so she wouldn't think that he just went away and came back changed. We waited at the airport a long time. When she saw him, she said, "Ooooh, Daddy, you look silly . . . really silly."

April 17, Manila

I am here alone with the kids in Manila. The Philippines is virtually closed down for Easter. We called Francie and Alex Tavoularis. They are about the only people from the production who haven't gone to Hong Kong for the holidays. We all played around in the pool and made Easter eggs. God, it is so hot.

April 20, Manila

Yesterday Francis sent a telegram to Secretary of Defense Donald Rumsfeld, explaining the situation and asking him why he couldn't rent equipment from the U.S. military the same way *Green Berets* did. He really needs a Chinook helicopter to lift the PBR [river patrol boat] into the river for that scene at Village II. The Philippine Air Force has no lifting helicopters. It seems like the Defense Department is exerting a kind of censorship. A film about World War II gets all sorts of cooperation.

I keep thinking that I must come up with a concept for the documentary. If I knew what the basic idea was I could be more specific about what to shoot. I guess I am counting on the concept eventually appearing obvious to me and being better than anything I could figure out in advance. I try to assess the moment and shoot what seems pertinent and feasible.

April 21, Manila

After all the countryside we've seen, I was surprised how beautiful and exotic the drive to Pagsanjan was. Maybe it was just the backlight, or my mood. I could see all the little details, as if looking at a mound of split-open coconuts drying at the side of the road, I could see each one individually. There were rice paddies, little villages of nipa huts, water buffalo, a family's wash drying on a graveyard fence, a slice of watermelon hanging from a string over a vendor's head, stripes of light coming through palm-frond roadside stands, stacks of cheese wrapped in neat banana leaf packages, a slatted-wood couch under a tree set back from the road as if people came to sit and view what was passing by, fields of sugarcane, and purple-blue mountains in the distance.

April 22, Manila

It is Roman's birthday. I let him stay home from school and go to the location today. We're waiting at the airport for this little single-engine plane to be serviced to make the flight to Baler. It's about an hour late so far, but I don't want them to rush. They have the engine cover off and are fussing around. Roman is lying on a desk here in the pilots' lounge. We got up at five thirty and now it is almost eight. It's real hot and we're starting to wilt. Hot and waiting. Those are the most descriptive words for most of the time here. Francis went ahead in the MU-2 jet with Vittorio and the crew. Roman and I, and my cameraman Doug, are waiting. I can't stop the thought crossing my mind: this little plane could go down.

We boarded the plane and the engine started up. I heard a second engine above and behind me. I felt immediately relieved. I hadn't seen it in the shadows of the hangar. The odd little plane is called a push-pull. It was painted light blue. The North Vietnamese used them. They camouflaged them against the sky since they had no air force to hide on the ground. We flew low. It was very beautiful, but bumpy. I felt sick, but at one point I was able to ignore my stomach and focus on the view. The rice paddies were laid out in incredible patterns. I could suddenly see what abstract painting is about. It is a kind of view of reality that does exist.

We passed over mountains denuded and eroding, where mahogany forests used to be. Finally, we banked around, came down low over the coconut palms on the valley floor and landed on a field of ruts and grass that is the Baler Airport. I noticed a little thatched hut had sprung up selling soft drinks. There weren't nearly as many kids watching us as there had been the first times we landed.

The helicopter was waiting and we were over the set in

another five minutes. It looked sad now that it was almost destroyed: charred bamboo skeletons of houses sticking out of the water. Smoke fires were already set on the beach for today's shooting. We landed on the sand and walked up to the village square to see what the first shot setup was starting to look like. They were rigging some palm trees to blow up behind the schoolhouse. It began to rain. No one seemed to notice except the extras who got under banana palms or in doorways to keep their costumes dry.

At lunch a birthday cake appeared for Roman. He cut the cake himself. The dull knife tore through the icing and ripped up hunks of cake and he served it to the crew with his hands. No one seemed to mind. It tasted good and was gone in just a few minutes, with a lot of fingers scraping the last of the icing off the cardboard base. One of the GI extras said to Roman, "Jesus, you have it great, being a millionaire."

The whole day was spent in painstaking rigging and rehearsing the scene in the village square where the helicopter lands and they load a wounded GI aboard. I tried to shoot the rehearsals with the helicopter landing. We were so close that the rotor blades blew dirt and sand and smoke so hard it lifted me and the tripod off the ground. Just before a shot I'd put a plastic bag over the camera and get under it. Doug would put his jacket over that and try to hold me down. Finally we gave up and got a shot from behind a sheet of Plexiglas, where one of the main cameras was. There were people's heads in my frame that I didn't want. The main shot, with all its complicated timing of effects, etc., didn't go until about 5:15. Vittorio was really upset because the helicopter didn't land in the exact same place it had during rehearsal, and his camera didn't get the composition he wanted. After talking it over, Francis decided to come back early tomorrow and try for it again.

When we got home to Manila we had a birthday dinner for Roman. Fred and Gray were there talking about if Jack Nicholson did the picture and they had to give him a percentage, how much each percentage point would be worth if the film made $40 million, and how much they would make if an unknown did the part, and how much if the picture made only $20 million, or if it did $80 million. All the while Roman was at the end of the table opening his presents: $11 swim fins, $1 poker chips, a $2 T-shirt, 15-cent comic books, a pelota ball and some little cap rockets.

April 23, Baler

The alarm went off at 4:43 A.M. and we were on our way to the airport at 5:30. I don't think anybody expected us to be on time. They were still fueling the plane, but we did get an earlier start than usual. We were on the set at 6:30 and the crew was there and beginning to reset the same shot as the previous day. I went back to the town of Baler to find Doug and Larry. We decided, since the setup was the same as the day before, we would use the morning to get some shots of the jeep trip from the town to the location. We chose a jeepney that was very typical, all painted with a silver horse on the front and a Jesus picture over the dashboard. We photographed along the road to the location. We kept asking the driver to stop and back up. After a while he got the idea of what we wanted to do and began teaching us the Tagalog words for stop, *hinto*; go forward, *avanti*; backward, *atrase*. It seems like a cross between Japanese and Italian. Finally, the driver said to me, "You very small, you husband very big. You very rich, Mr. Coppola very, very rich." It made me think of that day in the market in Manila when I wouldn't buy oranges because they were three for $2 and huge papayas were about 15 cents. My kids said, "Come on, Mom, you're rich."

When we got back to the set, the morning shot got off

early and well. Everyone was in a good mood. It was the first time since the beginning of shooting that the crew, camera, props, effects, direction, action, everything all just clicked together the way it was supposed to. One of the Filipino crewmen cut into the top of a palm tree that was on the ground after the effects explosions. He whacked through the layers of leaves and cut the heart out with his machete. A lot of people tasted it. I took a big chunk home and made a heart of palm salad with lots of olive oil, vinegar and garlic.

April 24, Baler

There are regular old-fashioned outhouses for the extras and six chemical toilets for the *cast* and *crew only*. Yesterday they ran out of chemicals. It was ten times worse than any outhouse. I nearly vomited.

I am sitting inside Francis's little thatched dressing-room hut. It is nice to be alone for a few minutes. The light is filtering through the woven mat walls, making bright little rectangles on my legs. The wind is blowing the palms outside. When I close my eyes it could be the sound of the wind in the pine trees at the mountain cabin at home. Maybe it's because the coconut palms are about the same height as pines. I can hear the voice of one of the military advisers in the hut a few feet away talking to Martin Sheen. He was cast as Willard on Francis's trip to L.A. This is Martin's first day on the set. He was at our house last night until curfew at 1:00 A.M. I was very impressed with his humanness. I tried to tell him that today and immediately felt awkward. We got up at 4:45 again this morning and now I am starting to fade. I don't know how Francis keeps it up. He made some espresso with lunch today, which helps.

April 25, Manila

We talked to Francis's parents on the phone. His mom asked me if the real reason Brando wasn't doing the film in May was because he was too fat. I said no, it was because the set wasn't ready and Brando wanted to spend the summer months with his kids. Later I realized how boring my answer was. No magic movie gossip.

April 26, Baler

We ate breakfast at 5:00 A.M. in Manila. Now it's 9:22 and I'm starving. I'm sitting here on these sandbags fantasizing about what I'd eat if I were in San Francisco. I guess I'd go to Mama's at Washington Square Park and have the works.

I don't even have any peanuts.

41

Cleaning out my purse/camera bag, I just realized that I haven't worn any lipstick for several weeks. I looked in the tube; it was all melted over to one side.

This morning we are waiting, because the Medevac helicopter wasn't called early enough. It was needed to stand by in case anyone was hurt in the big exploding stunt in the square. Now the light has changed. It is starting to sprinkle, and we have to wait for bright sun to match the shot from the other day. Francis is angry, but instead of yelling, he went over to the jet ranger and is taking a flying lesson. He is practicing hovering and landing. The wind must be carrying the sound some strange way; even though they are across the river above the rice paddies, it's very loud. The water buffalo are milling around.

Somebody broke into the wardrobe department yesterday and took the asbestos gloves the fire crew wear when they run in to get the suits off the burning stunt men. They sent someone to Baler to buy more; all they could find were bridal gloves.

———

On the set, it's very easy to get into a conversation about still cameras. Everyone seems to have at least one, or is deciding what additional equipment to get in Hong Kong. Nat was asking me about mine. The conversation got around to lenses. I said I only have one. He said, "What, a rich lady like you has only one lens? Even your driver has four." I had this little twinge as if I were doing something wrong. Actually, the photographs I want to take could be shot with an Instamatic. I'm interested in recording some moments that are in front of me. Just isolating out some things from all the rest, not making it beautiful or moody, or interesting; not judging it, only reporting what I see. Any camera would do. I like the one I have. I'm used to it. I'm attached to it. I guess I have the ultimate luxury: I have all I want.

April 27, Baler

As I was flying in the helicopter from the set to the Baler airstrip, I suddenly remembered how scary it was to go up in a helicopter those first few times. Today we were riding with the doors off and no seat belts, just holding on to the camera mount with one hand and balancing a stack of film cans with the other. It was about the same as traveling that route in the jeep, except a lot faster, not so bumpy, and the view was fantastic.

April 28, Manila

Francis had two readings with the cast this week. The actors were very enthusiastic, but Francis is really in a state of anxiety and fear that the script has some good supporting characters and some good scenes, but Willard and Kurtz are not resolved and here he is in the middle of this giant production. I remember the anxiety he felt and the struggle he had with the script of *Godfather II*, and it seems, in retrospect, at that time he was himself dealing with the same themes in his own life—money, power and family. Now he is struggling with the themes of Willard's journey into self and Kurtz's truths that are in a way themes he has not resolved within himself, so he is really going through the most intense struggle to write his way to the end of the script and understand himself on the way. He seems to

43

know that he will either get himself there and his script too or he won't, and it really scares him.

Looking back, maybe that is why he has struggled with all his scripts, starting with *The Rain People*. They are about themes he is in the process of working out within himself, rather than from things he has resolved and can be detached and objective about.

April 29, Manila

On the way back from Baler in the jet, I rode in the co-pilot's seat. The big side window was like my personal movie. We passed over the water. The delicate lines of the odd-shaped fish traps looked like giant Paul Klee drawings on blue-gray paper. Then we were over the edge of the coast. I could see the canals and the rows and rows of neat squares where the people farm salt by evaporating seawater. At one point we were in a cloud sandwich, with clouds above and below us; the plane, the mountaintops and the orange setting sun were in a clear space in the middle. Loud, screeching air traffic directions were coming over the radio as all the planes in the area prepared to land before dark, the deadline set by martial law.

More and more it seems like there are parallels between the character of Kurtz and Francis. There is the exhilaration of power in the face of losing everything, like the excitement of war when one kills and takes the chance of being killed. Francis has taken the biggest risk possible in

44

the way he is making this film. He is feeling the power of being the creator/director and the fear of completely failing.

April 30, Manila

This feels like the hottest day so far. As I left the air-conditioned bedroom, an invisible wall of hot air hit me with real physical impact.

The house here is wired for 110 and 220 current. Each plug has two outlets. The American appliances we brought plug into 110. Somebody blew out the toaster when we first got here and now I just blew out the electric coffeepot.

The espresso machine isn't working and the little pot that goes on top of the stove is up on the location. I am really in a grump. All I want is one good cup of coffee in my own home.

We are paying rent on this house like you would pay in Beverly Hills. It is big and comfortable for us, but the electricity goes off a lot, and now that the weather is really hot, the water is off more and more. It has been off all day today, the toilet won't flush and I can't take a shower. The neighbors tell us how lucky we are because we have a swimming pool and can at least get wet.

April 30, Manila

I think I've figured out why the people here have such beautiful complexions. They sweat all the time and it's very lubricating. My Irish skin needs a cool, damp climate to survive. I look all red and blotchy.

May 1, Manila

It is Labor Day here. No one is working except Francis and the editors. They are downstairs, bent over the editing table, looking through all the footage so far. There is about ten hours' worth and they have been at it about four hours now. On Labor Day, President Marcos grants some concessions to the labor movement here. Today's paper says he has raised the minimum wage in Metro Manila to 10 pesos a day, approximately $1.25, and farm labor to 7 pesos a day.

We were having lunch outside and Francis was telling these terrific stories about how he almost got fired during *Godfather I*, all the inside intrigue and a story about a real Mafia guy who was in the picture. I looked down through the glass tabletop. There were millions of tiny ants crawling all over everybody's feet.

46

The kids are downstairs playing Monopoly. They are playing with the French set. Park Place is Champs Elysées. Roman is translating the little cards that look like Community Chest. Marc is computing hotel rentals in francs on his calculator. It's not the way we used to play.

There are big brown cockroaches here. They don't seem to do anything, but they really bother me. Last night, when I took Sofia to the bathroom, there was a big one walking along the back of the sink across the toothbrushes.

May 2, Baler

The road from the little town of Baler to the set consists of two ruts worn in the sand by the production trucks and jeeps. Every day, several workmen lay palm fronds on the worst places to give the vehicles a little more traction. The ruts end at a lagoon. Some buildings with thatched roofs and woven mat walls have been built there to house the wardrobe, the makeup department and the long tables where lunch is served. The set and all the other equipment are across the lagoon. A stream of boncas and little motorboats ferry people back and forth. Today, two boats collided bringing people across for lunch. Those of us who weren't able to crowd into those first boats laughed at the people who fell in. There were two still photographers who dunked their cameras and were pretty upset. It looked as if

47

it would be a long time before another boat came, so Doug and I walked into the water, fully dressed, and made our way to the other side. It was up to my armpits at the deepest point. It was refreshing. My clothes stayed damp for several hours.

This afternoon, I shot my first interview. It was with Bobby Duvall. I was pretty nervous trying to look through the camera and talk with him at the same time. I wanted him to direct himself. I hoped it would be better than answering a set of preplanned questions. His character is a cocky air cavalry colonel who likes to wrap up operations early and go surfing with his troops. In the script, his helicopter unit attacks a coastal village and lifts Willard's boat into the mouth of a river at a place where the surf is good.

Bobby talked about basing his character on a West Point officer he knew: a guy whose life only made sense if there was a war. He talked about the details of his costume, the spurs on his boots, his ring, his belt buckle and Stetson hat. He took off his shirt. He was tan and hard. He had his belly sucked in. He ran his hands through his neatly cropped crew-cut hairpiece.

May 3, Manila

Yesterday was the first day of shooting that Francis didn't seem beaten and tortured. It's as though his exhilaration is building back. Today is Sunday. We went to the gambling ship in the harbor. It was old and sort of sweet. We played

48

with cash. People had stacks of pesos on the table in front
of them. It looked like Monopoly money. I played a slot
machine. I lost about $6. My hands were black from han-
dling the 50-centavo pieces. Francis played craps and built
up his stack of winnings to about 3000 pesos, but then lost
it and ended up about even. Marty played keno and lost a
little. His wife, Jan, had several good runs on the slot ma-
chines. Marc was the only winner. He won about 125
pesos, but I think he was more excited over the fact he got
in the casino, not being twenty-one. We came home
through the Sunday traffic. Vittorio, his wife Tonia and
their children were at our house making pasta and frittata.
Francis was happy and relaxed at the dinner table, speaking
Italian and enjoying all the kids. Around the table were
Francis; Vittorio's children Francesca, Fabrizio and Giovanni; Roman, Gio, Sofia and Marc; Jan and Marty Sheen;
Vittorio, Tonia and Tonia's sister Rita. Enrico came at the
end. We had a real American-style salad with avocado, blue
cheese, lettuce, oil and vinegar, garlic and purple onion. It
was a great change. The espresso machine seemed to be
working better. Francis made coffee and Francesca served
it. When she got to me she said very carefully in English,
"You want?"

May 4, Manila

I was looking at my footage on the editing table early this
morning when I heard this little out-of-tune voice on the
stairway singing "Happy Birfday to you." It was Sofia.
Today is my fortieth birthday. I feel pretty terrific. I looked

in the mirror and I do look thin. I have lost weight. I'm down from about ninety-nine to around ninety-three pounds. It made me think of a trashy story I read in a magazine a couple of years ago on an airplane. It was about this young stud and his exploits with beautiful girls, sometimes several girls at a time. One encounter he had was on a yacht, where this skinny old lady cornered him and he had to do this and that with her and how grateful she was. One of his lines was, "Jesus, she must have been forty years old." Actually, I feel more together, active, confident, than at almost anytime I can remember. My kids are terrific, I love my husband, I am fine.

May 5, Baler

On the way in from the airport, Doug and I stopped by a rice paddy to get some shots of a family planting rice. I wanted a view of what the company sees every day on the way to work. It was all very picturesque from the road for the wide shot, but then we started to walk out to where the people were for a close-up. Doug sank into the mud and the camera went down with me hanging on. It was pure mud with little narrow mud ridges between the paddies. We walked on top of the ridges. The mud was squeezing between my toes and I was trying to keep my balance and cursing because I was wearing my $25 leather sandals from home instead of the local 30-cent rubber thongs. We finally got set up. The shots were of a family standing in muddy water up past their knees. They were sticking little bundles of rice plants in the water at intervals. The tops of rice shoots floated in neat rows of green spots in the gray, muddy water. The people laughed at us with our tripod straddled over a ridge, the legs sinking deeper and deeper and me trying to keep my balance, not fall in, and operate the camera.

It was about 9:00 A.M. when we got to Baler and already superhot. I bought another straw hat. I guess I left mine on the plane. It's about 1.70 pesos, 20 cents, for a really nice handwoven hat. The lady knows me now and sort of laughs when I come in, because one day I asked her to show me what was in a box labeled crackers. It was in a glass case with hair tonic, buttons, baby powder, etc., and I knew it couldn't be food. It turned out to be caps for a cap gun, which was just what Roman needed for a little rocket bomb he got for his birthday. I bought the whole box.

I dropped in at the production office. Leon was yelling over the radiophone about how the production hired 110 security men, and there wasn't one on the set this morning. Only some little guy with his family, cooking rice over an open fire right near the gasoline storage tanks. All day yesterday, the Philippine Air Force general was on the set with some ladies in sundresses, sitting in the director's chairs, as if he had come to a spectator sport. The production is paying a fortune to rent the helicopters, and every day they send different pilots who don't understand the directions or who weren't flying during the rehearsal the day before. They don't fly in the right place, and wreck thousands and thousands of dollars' worth of shots. The helicopters flown by inexperienced pilots shows in the footage. American combat pilots just didn't fly like that.

The Philippine Air Force lost ten Hueys fighting in the south recently. They only have nineteen left in the whole country and are supercautious now.

We got to the set about 10:30. It was like a real war going on. The shot had started, so we had to watch from a distance. About eight helicopters circled and landed in smoke flares, ground rocket fire and water hits. Lines of GIs off-loaded and ran up the beach, crouching, firing and advancing. Between takes we got a boat to take us close to where the main camera was. We waded ashore with our gear and got up the beach, near enough to get some good shots of Bobby Duvall in his cavalry hat, taking the beach. He looked terrific, he knew it, and was real up and radiating energy. Everyone could feel it. There was a photographer from *Newsweek* who kept taking my picture every time I looked through my camera. I had that feeling of being merchandised: "Wife of FFC making movies too." I wanted to just pick up my stuff and walk out of there; I reminded myself that I am asking all the people on the production not to walk away when I'm shooting them.

1:30—set dressing is sprinkling bags of dry sand so the beach will not look so wet. During the last take, the water explosions rained down on everything. In the shot, there was green, purple and yellow smoke, bloody bodies, helicopters landing, GIs taking the beach and water explosions. Now the wardrobe department is changing the main actors into dry costumes. They're about ready for another take. The helicopters are warming up. The sky is gray with orange, casting unusual light. Everybody is excited and up for this shot. There are so many explosions. The ones in the lagoon are about 150 yards away; when they go off the beach shakes with a heavy tremor, like an earthquake.

2:00—I feel pretty confident now that I have made almost every mistake there is to make with my main camera. So I am not afraid to shoot a key scene myself. But just now I was using the backup camera. The helicopters were landing, the explosions were going off, I started to roll and all I could see was black. I couldn't figure out what was wrong. Doug was down the beach taking sound. Finally, I ran down to get him. By the time he helped me out, the scene was nearly over. I missed it all because some little iris I didn't know about was closed over the eyepiece.

May 6, Baler

Yesterday afternoon around three, I decided to get some
shots of David operating the Astrovision camera in the
MU-2 jet. Doug and I went out to the landing strip. The
plane had been sitting in the sun all day. When we got in,
it was like stepping into a sauna. We were wringing wet
with sweat in just a few minutes.

We took off and got above the clouds. David started looking for the Philippine F-5 fighters to photograph while they
rehearsed for tomorrow's shot of the napalm drop. The
camera was mounted on the belly of the plane. David op-
erated it by remote control as he looked at a video screen
inside the cabin. The copilot had a VHF radio pressed to
his window, trying to contact the jets. The pilot and David
were looking out both sides and yelling over their headsets.
The idea was to line up the MU-2 with the Philippine jets
and fly as close as possible at an angle so the camera could
photograph them. David would yell, "Where are they?
Where are they?" The cockpit would answer, "On the right
at nine o'clock." Then the jets would streak past on the left
in some other position entirely. David would leap out of his
seat, yelling and looking out both sides. We started swoop-
ing, banking and diving; at one point we came up over the
top at zero Gs and floated up a few inches out of our seats.
I started feeling sick. I looked over at Doug. He was white.
He had put our camera down. He said, "God, have you got
a plastic bag?" I had a little one that my tape recorder
microphone was in. I gave it to him. He started throwing
up. The bag was too small. The vomit splattered around. I
gave him an armrest cover to use. We continued banking
and diving and chasing the F-5s. There was nothing I could
do to get out of there. I was trapped. I was sitting in a pool
of sweat, feeling as if my body were coming apart and I
would vomit or have diarrhea. I thought of taking off my

blouse to throw up in. Finally I just gave up. The G force was so strong most of the time I couldn't even move my arms. I just kept saying, "I can make it, I can make it, I can make it, I can make it"—like a survival mantra. I opened my eyes from time to time and the ground was like a green wall, perpendicular to the window, with palm trees and huts just hanging there. Then it would slide away and there would be sand and water sideways, like changing wallpaper. The plane creaked and strained as the pilot pushed passed the redline limit, trying to keep up with the F-5s. Finally we leveled out and slowed down. I could see the jets streaking off in the distance and I heard our landing gear go down. When we landed and the door opened, I dragged myself out and just lay down on the runway. I still felt sick at midnight last night.

It is so hot, I started to feel weak. I got into a little patch of shade and am going to forget about trying to shoot for a while.

The sun has shifted a bit, and my left foot is out of the shadow. It feels like it is about to blister.

Everything is waiting because this scene was started yesterday, in the morning, when it was overcast. Now it is bright sun.

Special effects men are loading gasoline for the fires along the napalm line.

Some guy behind me is talking about Terry's wife's tits.

May 7, Baler

7:30 A.M.—on the beach location. Someone probably told this kid they didn't want to see any trash on the set. He is walking around with a stick diligently pushing the little pieces of cigarette wrappers, paper cups, etc. into the sand, out of sight. When the first helicopter lands, the wind from the rotors will blow it all into view again.

9:00—Bobby Duvall's girlfriend was on the beach, crying and saying she was going to walk into the surf and just keep going. I remember during the shooting of *Godfather II* how I was crying all the time. Now that seems so long ago, some distant melodrama of the past. I hope I am finally through playing victim in my life.

9:30—The child of one of the extras died yesterday. They are taking up a collection for him among the cast and crew. Yesterday, Alex's wife had a baby girl. Mauro's wife had a daughter two weeks ago. There has been a marriage between two people who met on the film.

10:00—A. D. Flowers is setting the special effects. He looks tired today. He had a temperature of 102 last night. The doctor said it was from too much sun. Now he is wearing a huge straw hat. He's in his late fifties and this is a physically grueling shoot. Almost everyone has lost weight. Josh was looking for a piece of string to hold up his shorts this morning. I have lost six or seven pounds myself. All I feel like eating in this heat is fruit. There are only two other women regularly out on the set. There are several hundred men. The flabby American men are getting tan and strong. The women look tired.

10:30—The wind is blowing the jet fuel exhaust from the helicopters toward us. It is nauseating. Everybody is really hustling because the F-5 jets are coming over at 11:00 A.M. They can only make three passes. On the third, they'll drop the canisters that look like napalm, and special effects will set off a huge fire in the palm trees using thousands of gallons of fuel. They set it from bunkers dug into the beach. Security has been tightened, but a bunch of kids snuck out on the set earlier this morning. They are praying they can keep everybody away. The big effects are really dangerous. There is an air of excitement and anticipation.

11:30—The napalm went off right with the jets, flying through frame, perfectly. I was about a half mile away by the second camera position. I felt a strong flash of heat. The Vietnamese extras on the other side of the lagoon must have really felt it. The special effects men were pretty pleased. Twelve hundred gallons of gasoline went up in about a minute and a half.

12:15—Bobby Duvall has to leave tomorrow night to fly to a film in England. Everyone is working fast because there is so much left to do before he goes. The Italians are moving the dolly track to a new position. Their work is like a sculpture. They're setting two sections, one long one, from the beach to the lagoon, across the sand about a hundred yards. They lay a foundation, a wooden framework held together with clamps. Aluminum track is put on top of that and leveled with wedges, then the dolly is set on the track and the camera mounted on it.

There is a discussion going on behind me between the stunt man and a military adviser. The next scene includes the shooting of a Viet Cong prisoner in the side of the head. The question is, how shall he fall? A bottle of blood and a tube are rigged to his back, so it's best if he falls backwards to cover it. The military adviser says if he got shot at that close range with a .45 pistol, it would blow his head off and it wouldn't make any difference which way he fell.

May 8, Baler

Doug, Larry and I went down to the beach where the crew was loading into a Huey to go to the set for today. The location was around a point several miles up the coast, inaccessible by road. The first helicopter didn't have room for us. There was nowhere to go when it lifted off. We crouched down over the equipment, caught in a blizzard of stinging sand, whipped up by the wind from the rotors. We got on the next one with our camera case, heavy tripod and sound equipment. We flew low. I was looking out the open doors, absorbed in the view of totally natural tropical coastline. We started to hover and descend. The Huey set down in about a foot and a half of water on a reef. Everybody jumped out. We were standing in the ocean a quarter of a mile from shore, holding our heavy gear up out of the water. The helicopter lifted off, whipping up the water into a spray that drenched us. I tried to get out of the way, and slipped. One of my rubber thongs floated away. The reef was rough and sharp under my bare foot. Finally, we just planted the tripod in the water and mounted the camera. There was something to see in every direction. The set was a wooden platform, built on an outcropping of rock several hundred yards farther out on the reef. The shore was extraordinary tropical foliage, rimming a white sandy beach. Perhaps what Hawaii looked like a few hundred years ago. I had a wave of sadness, as if I had looked into the future a moment and seen hotels and glass-bottom boats. We could hear the Huey coming again, so we picked up the tripod and began to move out of the way toward the set. It was difficult to wade, carrying the equipment over the uneven reef. The set seemed to be much farther away than it had looked at first. When we reached the rock, I was exhausted. I sat down on some boards and pulled off my wet jeans, glad I had happened to wear my bathing suit.

I am resting here, warming in the sun. The shot for today is an over-the-shoulder on Bobby Duvall, with the surfers riding the waves amid a barrage of water hits. This location was picked for its good surf. Today the sea is totally calm. There are no waves in sight. The special effects men have set explosives out on the reef. They are sitting near me, talking about how, after a few go off, there will be some dead fish around, and the sharks will come in. A cool breeze is blowing from the water. I can hear one of the stunt men talking about his house in Woodland Hills: "It's only two bedrooms, but the cabinets in the kitchen are all oak, and in the bathroom they are alder wood." Pete Kama is asking him where he ordered the cabinets, because he had custom cabinets made for his house and they didn't fit right.

May 9, Manila

The Italian crew ordered about $700 worth of groceries from Rome. It came yesterday and the shipping and duty amounted to $8000. When they found out they went bananas, so the production office sent the stuff to our house. About fifty cases were unloaded just inside our front door. We can hardly get in and out.

It is Sunday, people are dropping in—hanging out, coming swimming. There are people here every evening doing some business or other. The housekeeper's and baby-sitter's friends come by. The maid's boyfriend, the driver and the guard hang out in the back. I am starting to feel saturated with people. They are all nice. I have no reason to be heavy and chase anybody out. I just ache to be alone with only the kids and Francis.

May 10, Baler

Martin Sheen was telling me about adjusting to this location. So far, he got his face cut and had four stitches. He fainted crossing the street in Baler in the heat; they just sat him down in the middle of the road with the jeepneys whizzing by. When the boats collided taking people to lunch, his new camera was ruined. He said last night it had started to rain hard. He had plugged up the gaps in the screens in his room with toilet paper and he was trying to get it out so he could take the screens off and close the windows. He was dripping wet, the bed was wet. About the time he got settled into the other bed, the rain stopped and he had to get up and open the windows because the humidity was so intense. He had to replace the screens to keep out the mosquitoes. The only good thing was the dogs stopped barking when it rained. The dogs in Baler sleep during the heat of the day and bark most of the night, and the chickens start crowing about 4:30 A.M. Marty was talking about it all with some humor. Another actor would be screaming for his agent, demanding a list of working conditions.

Mona told me that yesterday the tiger that will be used in a scene arrived from L.A. It had been in a crate for thirty hours and the handlers were very concerned about it. They took it to the studio and let it out in the wardrobe room. It was lying down suffering from jet lag. It perked up at lunchtime and ate four chickens and a ten-pound roast. In the afternoon they took it out to the airport to put it on the DC-3 to go to Baler. The crate wouldn't fit through the door of the plane, so they walked the tiger on like a passenger. Four Italian wives, just in from Rome, were already in their seats. It took about an hour to calm them down. Then the pilot refused to get on. The plane was pretty late arriving in Baler. There was the usual crowd of kids and onlookers. The town has no TV. The production seems to be the local entertainment.

May 11, Baler

This morning Dennis told me the story about transporting the tiger on the airplane. He said that the passengers were in their seats when they put the tiger's carrying box on the plane. They placed a chicken by the door of the box, but when they walked the tiger on, instead of taking the chicken and going into it, he jumped on top of the box and was staring down at the passengers. Everyone ran into the front compartment and locked the door. The pilot climbed out his window onto the wing and just sat there, refusing to fly.

At two this afternoon, I think I was about as hot as I have ever been in my life. It was a huge effort just to move. I was mad at myself because I just couldn't get up to go down the beach to where the helicopter was lifting the PBR. When I finally got there, I missed the shot. My camera wasn't set up in time. The production couldn't get a big Chinook helicopter. They had to use a Huey. It lifted the PBR on long cables; it was too heavy. Instead of setting it down in the river, they dropped the boat in the lagoon and it split open.

May 12, Baler

This morning John told me the story about the tiger on the airplane. He said the pilot jumped out the window of the cockpit to the ground, which was a long way down. After they got the tiger into his box, the pilot refused to enter the regular passenger door and walk past the cage, so they had to get a ladder and he climbed up on the wing and in the window of the cockpit. He didn't come out until they landed and the tiger had been trucked away.

I am sitting on a couple of big leaves. The ground is still wet; it must have rained a lot last night. I am leaning against the trunk of a coconut palm. I just looked up. It's loaded with coconuts. I vaguely remember someone saying it could be lethal if one drops on you. Now that I look around, no one else is sitting under one. We are in a little clearing, surrounded by thick jungle foliage. Francis is sitting with the actors, rehearsing. We must be near the water because a hermit crab in a snail's shell is crawling by. Yesterday a young woman interviewed Francis on the set and said, "Now that you have accomplished so much and you're famous around the world, what possible challenge is there left for you?" Francis answered, "I am just trying to get through today."

He meant it. He has been superfrustrated by all the problems of the production. Now they still exist, but with the new staff in production there are others responsible and the focus for Francis has shifted to his own work. As long as his attention was on problems with helicopters, etc., the problems were huge, but objective. The last couple of days the work has been intimate with the actors where the focus is on the writing and directing. Francis has to confront himself. He works in a way that allows some incredible moments to happen, but it is risky and uncomfortable. Today he is waiting until the last minute to set the camera and dialogue.

We spent last night in Baler. We didn't plan to, they shot too late. The plane can't take off after official sunset—6:08 P.M. We stayed at the judge's house, which the production had rented for some of the actors. Janet and Martin Sheen had made a display for us on our dresser. There was a bottle of vitamins, one toothbrush and toothpaste, shampoo, shaving cream and a razor, deodorant, a bottle of some kind of body oil, cologne, a picture of the Pope and the Blessed Mother, a book of Chinese philosophy, one Trojan prophylactic, a clean shirt for each of us and a package of safety pins.

The generator which supplied electricity to Baler was destroyed in a typhoon ten years ago and never replaced. The production brought a new one but it doesn't supply the whole town. I took a walk. The streets were dark. Only the houses that have been rented for the cast and crew were brightly lighted. The other houses and little shops were lit by kerosene lamps and candles. People's faces flickered in and out of the shadows. I passed the tiger in a cage made of thick bamboo poles lashed together. It was on a truck parked in the road near the production office. Lots of kids were crowded around peeking through the bamboo bars.

62

Francis and I went to the Italian crew's house to have dinner. I was sitting next to Vittorio. He began talking to me about how he almost didn't take this film, because he had never worked on an American production and he was afraid that he couldn't be precise and definitive enough— maybe he couldn't do it the American way. At one point, Francis joined the conversation. He had been drinking a lot of wine and talking to someone else. He said, "Vittorio, I have a confession to make. I am scared every day that you will think I am an asshole, because I am not definitive enough, that I am trying to find my way, find the direction for this film."

Vittorio was speaking in English to us, and Francis was speaking Italian to him.

Earlier, Francis had been talking to Martin Sheen about how scared he was and that all the people on the production don't have any idea if the film is good or bad. He said, "In fact, if the crew thinks a scene is funny or someone thinks the rushes are great, watch out; because if something plays well by itself, that usually means that it is too complete and probably won't fit as a part of the larger whole film." He was telling Marty how, during the shooting of *Godfather I*, he was in the john, sitting on the toilet in a stall at the studio, and two crew members walked into the bathroom. They were talking about how the film was a load of shit and the asshole director didn't know what he was doing. Francis said he lifted up his feet so they wouldn't recognize his shoes. Now he feels that everybody on the production is looking at what he is doing, and saying to themselves, This is a load of shit, this is the director of *The Godfather*? It sure looks like nothing to me.

May 13, Baler

I take the kids to the set on Saturdays. Roman hangs out in the makeup department. He says he can make a bullet hit now as good as the assistant makeup man.

Today the company is shooting in a jungle area near town. At lunchtime we ate in the schoolyard. There were so many flies I fanned them away with my left hand while I ate with my right. The Filipinos didn't seem to be bothered. A woman at the next table was eating from two plates of rice; the flies looked like moving raisins.

I noticed the long, rough wood tables where we were eating were made of pure mahogany.

May 16, Manila

Yesterday was the last day of shooting in Baler. The company was working by the river with all the actors on the PBR and there wasn't really any good place for us to shoot. Doug went up on the tower where the second camera was and got a wide shot. Then we decided to go to the fishing village. I had heard people talking about it and had seen it from the helicopter. I thought it would be a long drive, but it was only about five minutes from the production office. We went in a yellow jeepney that was all painted up and had three silver horses on the hood. We got a couple of shots along the way of the little street stalls and people in windows. When we got to the beach it was the most naturally beautiful part of Baler I had seen. A village of bamboo and palm frond huts surrounded the mouth of a river where it met the sea. On the beach there were lines of people pulling on long ropes that extended out to fishnets in the water. The people were brown and smiling, and doing a sort of dance step in a rhythm as they pulled the nets. Higher up on the beach there were boncas, painted clear colors, blue and orange, purple, green and red. The people must trade fish for rice. They had little vegetable patches, chickens and pigs around their houses and coconut palms everywhere. It looked like paradise. Like you imagine Tahiti looked two hundred years ago. There were almost no signs of the Western world. There were no telephone or electric lines, no gas station, no hotel, no restaurant, no Coca-Cola signs. No clues that the rest of the world existed, except for some packaged goods in a roadside stand and a few plastic washtubs scattered near the houses. It was not hot like it is just a quarter mile inland; there was a breeze coming from the ocean. A bonca ferried people across the mouth of the river to a sandbar and little huts on the other side. The ride cost 10 centavos (less than a penny). There weren't even the two or three young foreign hitchhikers or expatriates you expect to find in a place like this just before the hotel scouts arrive.

We tried to shoot some footage, but the people crowded around us with such active curiosity we couldn't get enough distance to focus the camera. Some stood with arms linked and big cheese smiles, pointing at us to take their picture. Finally we put the camera back in the jeepney and just sat on the bluff. There were smiling, brown children playing with hand-carved wooden toy boncas in a little inlet in front of us. Coconut palms arched over thatched huts behind us. It looked like something out of a movie.

May, Manila

In many ways, living in Manila is like stepping back in time. For instance, plastic plants are really in; expensive, too. Real plants are very cheap. You can get a big potted palm for about $4, the kind you'd pay at least $50 for at home. Beautiful handwoven baskets are considered tourist junk; plastic products are preferred. Ice cream comes in beautiful tin containers that are discarded. Tea bags are made of cloth. Milk still comes in bottles that are returned. Frozen food seems to be on the verge of taking hold. I saw a few packages of frozen Birds Eye peas at the supermarket recently. They were $1.50 a package. Fresh Chinese pea pods are 12 cents a pound. One day I bought a bottle of California grapefruit juice. I thought it was 4 pesos; it was 40 pesos, which is about $5. Instant coffee is very chic. We were invited to the home of an Air Force general. After a very elaborate dinner, a servant brought around a silver tray with a silver creamer and sugar bowl and a large open jar of Maxwell House instant coffee.

May 18, Manila

The alarm went off early this morning. As I lay in bed, awake, I heard a voice in my head say, "Don't go today." I had arranged with Larry and Doug to go to Pagsanjan and shoot the progress on the set construction up there. I deliberated in my mind. Should I follow that voice, or be reasonable and go ahead with my plans? Finally, I decided that I could send them without me, and just see, this once, if that kind of information could possibly pertain to the regular world. I thought about telling Doug and Larry that I didn't feel well and wasn't going, but finally I got up my courage and, shaking with embarrassment, I told them the truth. They laughed and said that if it wasn't good for me to go, why should it be good for them? Maybe the bus would drive off a cliff or something. It was odd, but I felt very sure it was okay for them. Finally, they packed up the equipment and went without me. Around midmorning, I went up to the bedroom to be alone and try to understand what I was staying home for. It seemed like a perfect day to go to Pagsanjan. Francis was up at the set in Iba for the week. The kids were in school. There was no logical reason not to go.

About a half hour later, Francis walked in the front door. The PBR had broken down, he couldn't shoot. He was really angry; he had stormed off the set and flown home and said he wouldn't go back until there was a decent boat that worked. He just lay down on the couch and poured out all his anguish. I know he was glad I was home.

May 19, Manila

This is the first day of heavy rain. A typhoon is off the coast. I have never seen it rain so hard. I can barely see the palm trees in the backyard. I called the office and Francis left an hour and a half ago. It is only a ten-minute ride away. I am getting worried. The kids and I have nibbled away about a third of the roast, waiting for dinner.

May 20, Manila

The storm got more exciting. Water started coming in the rooms downstairs. In some places the carpet looked like it was floating because there was a layer of water between it and the pad. The kids thought it looked like a water bed and were jumping around on it. Pretty soon, the water was about six inches deep and it started out the bedroom door into the other rooms. Several people arrived from the office because the roads were so flooded they couldn't get home. It had taken them about two hours just to get to our house. We were all in the kitchen opening bottles of the Italians' wine when someone realized that the boxes of pasta were sitting on the floor downstairs in the water. Larry and Dean took off their shoes and waded across the room, and started carrying the cartons upstairs. Francis finally arrived. He had been stuck at some flooded intersection for the past hour and a half. He had gotten out to push the car and was completely soaked. The editors had been at the house all day, preparing a reel of film for a screening at Cannes. They decided it was hopeless to try to make it home. So, we began counting how many there were for dinner. There were fourteen, and the little half-eaten roast was about enough for four. Francis decided to make pasta. Since he is on his diet, he is always looking for a genuine excuse.

Sofia put on her raincoat and was running around in the

68

backyard. One section was underwater, and the frogs that usually hop around on the lawn there were all swimming. Sofia was chasing them and actually catching one now and then. The dirt from the flower beds was streaming into the swimming pool. Francis turned on *La Bohème* full volume. Marc, Roman and Gio were playing a noisy game of poker. The thunder and rain were so loud we were all shouting at each other. Finally, we did have a terrific dinner. As we got to the dessert, the electricity went off. We had bananas flambé by candlelight. After dinner Francis and I were sitting on the couch looking toward the table. There were three candles and a group of people at each end of the long oval table. Francis was talking about how fabulous our eyes are that they can compensate for the low level of light and see perfectly clearly. You could never shoot in that amount of light. It was really beautiful. Francis was marveling at how the people at the table were so perfectly staged. Now and then someone would get up and go to the kitchen and cross behind or in front of the light. Each person was so perfectly placed, leaning a little forward or a little back, catching the light. Making shadows on the wall behind, and silhouettes in front. He said you could never get it as good if you staged it. After a while we went to bed. I guess the rain stopped for a bit and everybody decided to try to go home. They started out, they got to the main road and had to turn back. The electricity came on at about four in the morning, and *La Bohème* started up, loud. The espresso machine began steaming, all the lights went on. I went downstairs to shut things off. People were sleeping all over the place.

May 21, Iba

This morning we came up to Iba. It was about a twenty-five-minute flight from Manila. The production will be located here for the next six weeks. It is on the coast but it is not as beautiful as Baler. Maybe it just seems that way because the weather isn't good today. The light is gray and the wind is blowing sand across the flat beach into the equipment trucks and eating area.

2:00 P.M.—At lunch, the assistant director was calling for forty volunteers to help out because the camera barge broke its moorings and the PBR is dragging anchor. The typhoon is still coming toward us. The rain is picking up; so is the wind. The sheets of plastic on top of the thatched roof covering the dining area are starting to whip around. The sandbags aren't holding them.

3:00 P.M.—The weather report says winds of sixty miles per hour are expected. I can hear directions going over the walkie-talkies to tie everything down. The rain has really started. I can't see across the open yard where the trucks are parked. It's a gray-white wall of water. The wardrobe man is on the radio. The tents, where he has costumes for eight hundred extras, are blowing away.

May 22, Iba

I am sitting in a reception room of our hotel. Francis is rehearsing. The chairs and couches have white carved wood frames with gold spray antiquing. The upholstery is orange-flowered plastic. The curtains are avocado green. There are two large arrangements of artificial flowers, one with plastic sunflowers, the other with sprays of colored fake wheat. There is a white piano, several black and one turquoise ashtray. There is a hi-fi in a console and a round coffee table with V-shaped wrought-iron legs.

I feel as if I have seen this exact room somewhere. Maybe in an interior design book during the fifties. It was the "before" room. Danish modern was the "after."

Medavac set—4:00 P.M.—I am in a tent, sitting on an operating table. It is raining off and on. It is cool, thank God. I can hear the pumps, pumping river water to flood the area around the tents. The road is out. Everyone walked out here through the mud. Most of the local people are barefoot. I sank into the mud and my sandals just stuck there. A guy had to pull me out. It's teatime here in the tent. The Italian crew is talking and sipping espresso.

5:00 P.M.—The wind is getting stronger. Stuff is sliding across the floor.

Some young extras are standing near me. They are talking about their GI haircuts . . . how long it would take to grow back . . . about blackjack . . . about money they get paid . . . how it's $25 a day and they haven't done anything, just wait around. Three hundred extras went back on buses today.

May 23, Iba

I am sitting in the helicopter. Francis is going around the outside with the pilot, checking out everything to be sure there was no damage in the storm last night. It is just like sitting here in a car, except the visibility is better. They are taking the sandbags off the skids. Gray just drove by and said we were lucky we stayed in Iba. There was no water or electricity at the hotel in Olongapo last night and everybody went in the swimming pool with bars of soap. Several people stayed in the pool most of the night. The air conditioning was off and the rooms were like saunas with mosquitoes.

———

Bill Graham is here to play the part of the Playboy bunnies' manager. He was telling me how he has this suite with a great view that he always stays in at the Park Lane Hotel in New York, and in London he stays at the Savoy. He says he has earned the right to be very particular about his accommodations, his staff knows it and always books him the best. Because of the typhoon, the last four nights he has had neither running water nor electricity at any of the hotels where he stayed. Bill was telling me about telephoning his office. How he is used to talking on the phone all the time. He said when the phones were out in Manila he just sat there and dialed and dialed anyway. He said his office expected him to be fired after the first day of shooting for insubordination. They were sure he could never work for anybody else. He asked me why Francis had wanted him for a part. He said he was so intrigued by Francis asking him that he fit it into his heavy schedule. He had to have a whole convention rescheduled where he was the keynote speaker.

———

This is the second day of waiting inside the Medevac tent. I have taken all of the photos I feel like taking. I am tired of chatting. Dick White gave me a whole lecture on helicopter maintenance, what you look for and safety statistics. He told me a story about landing in a little village a few months ago, up in the mountains, one evening in bad weather. He came down in a churchyard. The church was locked and abandoned. The names of the people who had made offerings some Sunday in September 1974 were still on the door. He said most of the offerings were about 25 centavos; 50 centavos from one person was the highest. (That's about 6 cents U.S.) Some people came out from underneath the church where they were living and he got to talking. They invited him to eat and sleep there. He said they gave him some red rice wine that was served in a bowl like soup. The rice was still in it. You spooned out the rice and then drank the wine. He said they got terrifically drunk, but had no hangover the next day. He bought three bottles to take home. They kept the bottles buried in the ground and dug them up for him.

I keep thinking of all the things I could be doing if I were home in Manila. I am not helping Francis, I am not shooting myself. I am just waiting in this limbo. I am in this tent. There are six Vietnamese children here. A bunch of props. Operating tables, cases of U.S. beer cans, Foremost ice-cream cartons, makeup supplies. One of the GI extras is shaving. There is an empty TV console, a table with tea, coffee and soft drinks. There are compressed-air tanks. Some men are bringing in bed frames and stacking them. There are bottles of IV fluid. A big American propman has picked up a little Filipino and is pretending he is going to drop him in the mud by the door. Some tables are being put down the center. I guess they are getting ready to serve lunch in here. A nurse has set up at the end of the table I am sitting on. She has a little lineup of men already. A cut finger, a headache, a splinter, a rash, etc. I tend not to want to look at the problems people are having. Outside

73

the door, Dean is fighting with the new propman. I can hear, "Well, fucking go home then." Gray is trying to arbitrate. I guess the propman quit.

———

Joe Lombardi is riding the tractor like a cowboy, pulling the helicopter mock-up down the road toward the set.

———

A skid broke off the helicopter and hit Joe in the foot. Everyone is crowded around him.

———

Paint department men are mixing up mud in helmets and splattering it on the walls of the Medevac hospital.

May 23, Manila, Evening

We came back from Iba in the helicopter despite the storm warnings. The pilot said we could start out and if it got bad we'd just come down beside a road and hitch a ride to a hotel for the night. We were flying low. There was a sensation of moving very fast that you don't get when you're way up there. The ground was like a rear-projection screen, changing to sea, beach, houses, rice paddies, hills and mountains. Then we were over an area of many giant ponds with low dikes all around. Occasionally there would be a wide place in a dike with a house on a tiny patch of land completely surrounded by water; or a little town of maybe four rows of twenty houses on a fifty-foot-wide strip with only bonca boats for communication with the rest of the world. I had always thought this area was rice paddies in the flooded stages, but the pilot said that they were fish farms, with around forty thousand fish in each pond. They raise shrimp and crabs there, too. People came out of their little huts all along the way and waved up at us.

When we got to Manila Harbor, it was raining heavily and there was a strong wind. The helicopter seemed to be flying sideways. We could see several boats broken apart in the rough sea below us.

May 24, Manila

It has been raining in Manila for five days now. The backyard is under about a foot of water. The landlord came over and removed the soggy carpet from downstairs. It was really starting to smell. Cecilia is trying to sweep the water out the side door or into the drain in the bathroom floor.

The electric pumps that pump city water to this area have been out for four days. We have no running water in the house. I went out in the rain this morning and got a bucket of water out of the swimming pool. I brought it to the bathroom to brush my teeth and wash my face. It took two more buckets to flush the toilet.

I took the kids to a department store to get some tennis shoes. It took nearly three hours. I couldn't figure out the system right away. First, you pick out a sample of the shoe you want and take it to a counter where you wait your turn to have a girl call for your size. After about fifteen minutes, a boy brings your shoes out and you try them on. Since it took about thirty minutes to get that far, you really think twice about deciding they're not right. You say yes, and a young woman writes up a bill in triplicate, shuffling carbon papers. Then she rings a bell, and in a little while a young man comes and takes your money and the bill off somewhere. Eventually he returns with your change and a claim check. You take the claim check to another counter and

wait in a line to claim your package. The shoes were all
on the mezzanine, but the maze of display counters and
ordering-your-size counters and writing-up-your-bill and
wrapping counters were not designated that I could see. It
turned out that my rain boots were in the women's department, Sofia's tennis shoes in the children's, Roman's in
boys' and Gio's in men's, with a different set of counters for
each. At one point, I was peering over the balcony to the
floor below, speculating about how long and how many
carbon papers it would take if I threw myself over and had
to be removed. I sat down in a chair and wept like a fool
for Macy's and my credit card.

May 25, Manila

It is really raining hard. The wind is blowing and whipping
the palm trees against the house. It looks like one of those
tropical storms you read about, but I don't remember their
mentioning the noise. We have to shout at each other.

It is fabulous to be cool, but now we are totally damp.
Everything is limp and starting to mold.

Sunday night, Francis, Bill Graham and the Italian crew
left at midnight in the bus to drive back to Iba. The plane
can't fly in this weather. It took eight hours to make a
four-hour trip and they finally had to stop because the road
to Iba was washed out. They didn't get to shoot yesterday
at all, so I imagine Francis's humor is grim.

I was in the office. It was like command headquarters,
with the production staff bent over maps trying to figure

out what to do. There is no telephone line to Iba. The company set up a man with a radio who taps out messages in Morse code, but now that's not working either. They wanted to coordinate getting some trucks up to where the road was out and ferry people across by bonca. The road to the set in Pagsanjan is out and the PBR replacement on a truck from Baler to Iba is stuck in some mountain village. There is no communication between any points.

May 26, Manila

This is the eighth straight day of rain. I have just made Sofia and her friend some play dough in the kitchen. They are singing "Jingle Bells," and Sofia is making this terrific Santa and sleigh with a reindeer and snowballs.

The office called and said that the whole company is coming back to Manila. The sets at Iba have been wrecked by the storm. Francis will probably be home this evening if they can find a way to get him back. They are ordering tickets to send people home to L.A., New York and Rome. The production is closing down.

6:00 P.M.—Mona just called and said not to expect Francis. They are shooting the Medevac set tomorrow after all. A helicopter got through and took Francis and the camera crew to the set at Iba. Francis wants rain for the Medevac scene, so now they are hoping that it continues through tomorrow. Mona started to tell me about the insurance adjuster coming in from Singapore to assess the typhoon damage, then she said there was either a mouse under her desk or a cockroach big enough to saddle and she hung up.

May 27, Manila

Luciano is this huge Roman with a big mane of hair. He looks like a gladiator. He was over Sunday with his wife. They just adopted a two-day-old Filipino baby. He sat in Francis's chair, holding his son, really beaming. The baby weighs less than five pounds. He barely filled the palm of Luciano's hand. They named him Fabrizio.

Maureen, the woman next door, took her little girl, Claire, Sofia and me to see a dance troupe from Mindanao. They performed in a small ballroom in a hotel. We were sitting at a front table. The program began with rather athletic dances, using fake spears. The long handles seemed to just miss our heads and occasionally one would hit the wall of the little stage. I was hoping to see some great fabrics in the costumes. There were a few, but the most beautiful handwoven skirt and head wrap would be worn with a polyester blouse that looked like it was right out of Woolworth's.

The event was sponsored by the Organization of American College Women in Manila. It was the first time I had been in a room filled with Western women since I left San Francisco. I kept looking around at what the women were wearing, how they did their hair, what kind of shoes they had on. I'd catch myself and focus back on the dancers. It surprised me that my eyes would wander away again to look at the other women.

May 28, Manila

I just made myself some Cream of Wheat. The first bite startled me. It was so hot. I had forgotten how long it had been since I ate any really hot food. A cold mango is about the ultimate here.

The taste of the Cream of Wheat reminded me of being pregnant and nauseated. It was the only thing I ate for months then. Today I feel sick and ache all over. I would think it was jungle rot or something exotic, but I have been here in Manila for the last five days.

God! I just weighed myself. I weigh eighty-nine pounds. I haven't weighed that little since I was fourteen. My mother wrote recently, she read somewhere that white women aren't suited to the tropics and were traditionally sent home.

One of those giant cockroaches just came up over the end of the bed and crawled along the spread. That's just about it for me. I can barely tolerate them in the kitchen and the bathroom. Janet Sheen said she woke up one night in Iba with one crawling on her face.

May 29, Manila

I just realized how much I am enjoying this evening by myself. Sofia went to stay all night next door. Gio and Roman went to the movies with Marc, and they're going to take a taxi home. They think it's some fun, scrambling to get back before curfew.

Francis is up in Iba. He is the only one I am worried about. He is so exhausted by everything. He is on some brittle edge. He has been shooting the last few days hip deep in mud, wet all the time. Tonight he is meeting with the lawyer and the production staff to assess what to do in the wake of the typhoon. Mona went up to Iba today with the insurance adjuster and said Francis definitely wants to shut down the production for some weeks. Francis is not a quitter. I wonder what his plans are.

This morning I noticed a piece of notepaper by the coffee machine with various numbers in red pen. At the bottom it said that the production is now six weeks behind and two million over budget.

I have just read Bob Dylan's name in *Time* magazine. It made me think of a night he came to our house in San Francisco. I got this actual pang of embarrassment sitting here, halfway around the world, a year later. He came with Marlon Brando and some people after Bill Graham's concert. Francis made a huge pot of spaghetti with olive oil, garlic and broccoli. I was in the kitchen getting things and everyone sat down at the table. Bob was hanging up his jacket or something. When he got to the dining room, all the chairs were filled except one next to the children down at the end, so he sat down there, not near his wife or Marlon or Francis. He sat there looking real glum and about halfway through he got up and left. I tried to tell myself he was tired from the concert and probably wasn't hungry. But I kicked myself for not being a smooth hostess. I am never comfortable with groups of people that I don't know, and yet I am constantly in the midst of spontaneous dinners of ten or fifteen people, many of whom are strangers. I suppose if I ever really learn to relax and enjoy it, Francis will decide to become a hermit.

There used to be a woman who called me once in a while and said, "Ellie, tell me, who was at your house for dinner last week?"

A famous person I don't know is like an unfamous person I don't know; I feel shy and uncomfortable, maybe more so.

————

I've been in bed all day today, really feeling lousy. Lots of little random thoughts have passed through my head. Something made me think of my friend Theo and the time she told me that all together she was responsible for thirty-two bathrooms . . . the house in Cleveland, the one in Sun Valley, the ranch and their San Francisco home. I remember laughing, because I was in the big house in San Francisco and I thought six bathrooms was a lot. Now I guess I'm up to about twenty-seven, if I count our places in Los Angeles, New York, San Francisco and Napa, plus this house here in Manila.

———————————————————

May 30, Manila

Francis came back today. Bill Graham was with him. He said they passed over the same area of fishponds we saw last week. The typhoon had knocked the little huts off the dikes and hundreds of people were stranded in the rubble. There seemed to be no indication of any government rescue operation. Francis and Bill started to talk about what they had been through the past five days. At Iba, the Medevac set was completely blown down. The PBR had been tossed up the bank, about forty feet, into the first line of tents. The speedboat was up on the helicopter pad. The river had risen a huge amount and washed away the piles of supplies near the dock. The generator truck was half under water and probably ruined. The dolly track was buried in four feet of mud. Everybody pitched in, hauled sandbags, dug through mud, and they actually shot Friday and Saturday.

June 5, Manila

I have been feeling crummy and nauseated for about a week now. I have never felt nauseated and tired, except when I was pregnant. Today I had a whole elaborate fantasy about what if I were pregnant. I thought about how many hours I have spent thinking about what if I really were pregnant. There was even one period when I thought heavily about why I wasn't pregnant. I wondered, on an average, how much time a woman spends thinking about those questions.

I heard about this doctor who had cured some of the people from the production who came back sick from Iba. He is Filipino; I've been seeing a European doctor. I asked him to come over and take a look at Francis and me. When he arrived, he ignored me and did a big number on Francis. The main point of his diagnosis was that we are dehydrated and lack salt. He said his miraculous cures for the crew consisted of intravenous feeding. As soon as he left I went to the kitchen and had two slices of watermelon, loaded with salt, and maybe it's in my head, but I do feel better.

June 8, Manila Airport

6:00 P.M.—We have been sitting on the plane now for about forty-five minutes. We boarded this flight expecting to depart for San Francisco. There were a lot of police with automatic rifles at five or six points between the terminal and the plane door. In the past month, there have been two rebel hijackings to draw attention to the civil war. We have not left the ground. The PA system announced that the delay is due to a problem in the external power source. The lights are off, except the exit signs. The air conditioning is off. People got on the plane with a certain decorum. Now they are unbuttoning their shirts and fanning themselves with their menus.

We are going home because the production has closed down for six weeks. The entire company is moving to Pagsanjan. It is about two hours by car from Manila over paved roads. Everything will be consolidated in one location. The sets that were destroyed in Iba will be rebuilt near Pagsanjan. We left our Manila house, too. Robin stayed to move us. We are going home until the production is ready to shoot again.

7:30 P.M.—We were deplaned. I am sitting in one of those molded plastic seats in the airport terminal. There is something about this waiting room. It could be anywhere. Once on a flight to Rio, I had been flying all night. I was awakened and herded into a terminal. There were no distinguishing features. I saw a lot of Japanese tourists and I had a sinking sensation. Perhaps I had taken the wrong plane. I searched for some clue as to what country I was in, where in the world I was. It turned out to be Lima, Peru.

8:30 P.M.—The PA system is announcing that the flight to Los Angeles has definitely been canceled. "The departure

of Flight 865 for Bangkok and Europe is now boarding."
There is still no word about our Flight 106 to Honolulu and
San Francisco.

9:15 P.M.—Our flight has been announced. The estimated
time of departure is 10:15. The clock on the wall says 2:30.

I am at the point where I've started noticing the spots of
chewing gum permanently flattened on the floor and waxed
over.

My eyes are starting to burn from the cigarette smoke
recirculating through the air conditioning.

I'm always saying that we make our own reality, so when
I get stuck like this I have to say I'm somehow choosing it.
Now's when that philosophy all breaks down for me. I'd be
in a better humor, maybe, but we just got out of the hospital
this afternoon. Francis and I did not feel better, so the
doctor sent us to the hospital three days ago. We had a lot
of tests and continuous intravenous feeding. The doctor
said our test results looked like we'd been in a concentration
camp for six months. We were dehydrated and had signs of
malnutrition. We stayed in bed in the hospital with tubes
in our arms until Francis got so antsy he got up and told
them to unhook the bottles and we walked out. The room
was rather like a motel room, with indoor/outdoor carpet
and Muzak. It had a sitting area and a bedroom part with
an accordion divider. We had twin electric beds and Francis spent long periods of impatience pressing the buttons to
elevate the feet, or head, or just ride up as high as it would
go and back down again. We checked in Monday night,
and Tuesday morning, when I woke up, Francis's bodyguard was sitting on the couch, reading the telephone
book. It took me about a half hour to get up the courage to
ask him to sit out in the hall.

A little nurse gave me a sponge bath in bed. She was very
discreet, and covered each part of me as she finished washing, maintaining modesty at all times in front of the man
in the next bed. I started fantasizing about what she was
going to do when she had to wash Francis. When she finished my bath she said, "Thank you berry much," and disappeared. A male orderly came in to bathe Francis.

June 8

It's been about twenty-four hours since we left our house in Manila. We're flying the last leg: Honolulu to San Francisco. Sofia has fifteen blankets and a stack of pillows spread over three seats next to me. She is playing house with a little girl about four. They are getting pretty hyper. Roman has the headphones on. He has learned the order of the music on the different stereo channels. *The Godfather* sound track on Channel 11 is followed by a quick switch to Channel 3, just in time for music from *The Sting*. Now, Sofia has made a little face out of chewed-up gum stuck to a piece of paper. She has rolled a tiny mouth, two eyeballs and a sort of snake for hair. She is drawing a body on the paper to go with it.

June 13, Napa

We woke up here in this colorless little house. Francis opened the door and it looked just like when Dorothy opens the door into the Land of Oz. There is a glistening pond with water lilies, a little island with a weeping willow and a big green bullfrog. There are flowering trees, sculptured hedges, Japanese maples with tinted leaves. Sofia went running along the little paths in her funny-footed pajamas, like a Munchkin. To the right, the manicured vineyards stretch up the hill to the eucalyptus and giant oaks, and behind that are redwood trees. It is like the point where the dream world and the real world meet. I feel complete and at home and truly "There's No Place Like Home." Manila seems like part of some former lifetime.

Mid-June, Napa

Last night we opened a bottle of 1889 wine that Francis got out of the boarded-up section of the cellar in the big house. The cork was all crumbly. Bob Mondavi was here and Mike, and each expert had a different idea about how to get the old cork out. It took about a half hour to remove it completely. They looked for something to decant it in. There was only a large peanut butter jar. The wine was still good.

June 20, Napa

Saturday I felt desperate to be alone. I felt like crying. I couldn't think of one thing to cry about. I wanted to just

walk away, up the hill behind the house by myself, but I
had to oversee the kids doing the dishes and straightening
up. It is amazing how we have all become total slobs, dropping everything everywhere. Living in this tiny cottage is
quite a change from having four people waiting on us in
the big house in Manila, although I love it here with just
us. It was around noon when we got everything in order,
and I was ready to step out the back door when people
started to arrive. Friends came to picnic. I started this conversation in my head about how could I possibly say I
wanted to go off by myself. I finally got up my courage and
excused myself. I had a terrific walk up an overgrown road
that ended at two faded old water tanks. Between the trees
there was a view back down to the valley. I could see the
neat rows of vineyards and the hills on the other side. I sat
up there for a long time. I saw a jackrabbit, several wood-
peckers, a blue jay. The water tanks were made of beautiful
weathered boards that had once been red. The kind of
wood you'd see in a photo of some chic New York apartment "country" kitchen. In the back of my mind I kept
wondering if family and guests were getting annoyed with
me.

June 21, Napa

Francis was reading a book about the life of Genghis Khan,
making notes into the recorder, and muttering about Kurtz.
The kids and I went to the cheese store. We got some
terrific ash Chèvre, a burgundy Cheddar, ripe Camembert,
some soft French cheeses I never heard of that were in the

case with the Boursin, and some Gruyère. When we got back, Gio picked grape leaves, and we laid the cheeses out on the breadboard among the leaves. We took a picnic, fruit, bread and cheese, out on the lawn, under the magnolia tree which is in full bloom. Francis opened a good Cabernet Sauvignon; the kids drank it, too.

June 24, Napa

Yesterday Mike and Arlene saw two hours of rushes, and when they called to ask us if we would like anything from the city, Arlene said she thought the acting was kind of tentative. Francis went into a tailspin. He felt totally defeated. He has spent $7 million, and months of grueling production, and they didn't say, "Hey, you've got some fantastic stuff there." He really got into a black depression. As I see it, Francis has ninety hours of film, and no chunk can give you an idea of what fifteen minutes' worth of moments he is going to select from it. What you finally see on the screen does not give the slightest clue of what was left out. For someone to just look at an arbitrary piece is meaningless. Francis felt hopeless and scared.

We slept outside on the lawn. It was a beautiful night, so clear with stars. Francis tossed and turned most of the night, having nightmares. We woke up at dawn; there was a crescent of new moon rising near the horizon in the pinkish light. Francis said he had had a dream about how to finish the script, but now that he was awake it wasn't really any good. Francis talked to Brando on the phone yesterday. He knows he will be great if he feeds him the right material in the script. We talked about all the fears plaguing him, and mostly they seemed related to the fact that the script isn't finished. He has been reading, researching, talking, thinking, writing and wrestling with it every day for almost a year now. I suggested he just dictate the whole thing, right now, complete, off the top of his head. He has struggled with it so long. He knows the material backward and forward. He is practically chasing his tail.

He is in there now with the tape recorder. He started at the beginning and is going straight through. God! I hope.

June 26, Napa

When Francis talked to Brando, he said he asked about me and the kids. I've actually only met the man briefly twice. The six weeks he was working on *The Godfather*, I didn't go to the set because I was pregnant. I had Sofia during those weeks. I went to the party the last day he worked. We were introduced; I had the baby with me. She must have been about two weeks old. He picked her up and marveled at her little toes and examined her long fingers. I felt that he was completely comfortable with her. There were no expectations, no pretensions, no bullshit, she just was. Francis is like that. He likes little kids. He'll talk to any little kids and get them to play with him. They have no preconceptions about him and movies. It's a relief.

I even notice it myself. When I am cashing a check or using a credit card, people often ask me if I am related to Francis Ford Coppola. Sometimes I say I am married to him. People change before my very eyes. They start smiling nervously and forget to give me my package or change. I think I look fairly normal. I wear sweaters and skirts and boots. Maybe they are expecting a Playboy bunny. I don't know. Last year I was buying a Honda car and the salesman was all bored, business pleasantries. When he wrote up the contract and found out what my name was, he got totally flustered. Finally he asked if he could ask me a personal question. I said yes. He asked, with real concern, why I wasn't buying a Porsche or a Mercedes. I told him that I drive almost exclusively in San Francisco and I thought the Honda was the best car for that. I could see my answer didn't satisfy him.

July 1

I am at my mother's house in Southern California for a couple of days. Francis had to go to Los Angeles and meet with the lawyers and United Artists and sign the loan deal. The film is $3 million over budget, which United Artists now has to put up, but Francis has to personally pay it back if the film doesn't make $40 million or more. That just makes me get all the more focused on the present moment and not waste right now thinking about all the "What ifs" of the future.

My mother has lived in the same house since the day she was married. Everything is familiar and almost everything has changed. The old road used to have potholes filled in with tar that would melt on hot summer days, and you could press things in it that would stay there for years. Now there are gleaming, concrete one-way streets with diagonal parking. We took the kids to Disneyland. I went once seven or eight years ago and I thought it was a monument to California commercialism. This time I thought it was great. It had some of the best art events I've seen anywhere. I've seen artists' holograms in galleries and museums, but Disneyland had fabulous holograms in the haunted house, much better than I've ever seen before. The fire effects in the pirate ride seemed like the reverse of filmmaking. Francis sets real fires and films them and then the celluloid reality moves past the stationary spectator. On the pirate ride, there were real celluloid fires and the spectators moved past.

I realized that I am not often in a large crowd of people at what would be considered a tourist attraction. I was amazed at how many people had cameras and were taking pictures everywhere. As the parade of historical events went by, Sofia was really into it, especially when she recognized "Christopher Crumbolus." I couldn't take my eyes off the people with their cameras. The real experience they were having was taking pictures, not being at a parade. There was a man on the opposite curb, aiming a Nikon with a long lens. He seemed to be taking pictures of me and the kids. The housewife with the children at Disneyland.

July 23, Hong Kong

We are on our way back to the Philippines and are staying in Hong Kong at the Peninsula Hotel. We were taken to the same suite we had stayed in before. It is different now; there are thick metal straps over the big view windows on the harbor side. The bell captain apologized, saying there was a typhoon 350 miles off the coast and moving in. He hoped it would not be necessary to board up the windows completely. There was champagne on a tray and fresh flowers. The bouquets were made of roses and a flower I had never seen before; someone had carefully folded each petal in half and tucked the tip down inside to reveal the large, elaborate centers. The flowers had no smell. The arrangements were placed on top of the television sets. I thought of the photos I took of the flowers on top of the television set in our room in Belgrade and in Brasília. I guess, the world around, they figure that you're going to be looking at the television for sure and will see the flowers.

This suite must be one of the most spectacular in the world: big rooms with beautiful views, grand marble bathrooms with Vitabath, terry-cloth robes and a cut-glass jar of cotton balls. Sofia disappeared into the bathroom for a long time. I went to look for her. She had made a cotton Santa's beard and mustache and was looking at herself in the three-way mirror.

There is a manservant who attends this suite exclusively. His name is Kong. He served jasmine tea when we arrived and opened the champagne. In the morning he took our breakfast order and brought the food and laid it out at the big dining table. He is attentive without being obtrusive. He has a graying crew cut and one, seemingly eight-inch-long, silver hair extending out from the side of his clean-shaven chin. He is very friendly with the children and played school and card games with Sofia while we went shopping.

Hong Kong is the supermarket of Asia, like Las Vegas is the gambling center of the United States. Every aspect of the city is focused on one thing, buying and selling international products. The neon signs say Sony, Sanyo and Gucci, instead of Golden Nugget and Caesars Palace. Francis loves to look at all the new products and gadgets. He went to see all the cameras and tape recorders and equipment in the stores. I went to two places where they sell products from Mainland China. I love the incredible

92

embroideries, especially the old ones. I asked the clerks to take out all the stacks. They were very indifferent and could hardly wait until I finished so they could continue chatting with the other clerks. They were clearly not getting any commission on what they sold. They yawned politely and told me certain stacks were too expensive, that I wouldn't want to see them. When I left the store I was annoyed that I hadn't insisted on seeing the expensive ones. I noticed that I liked some of the cheap items, like a woven basket or a kite for a dollar, or a fabulous antique vase or embroidery that cost thousands, and almost nothing in between. I thought of a therapist who once told me that I should buy more expensive things for myself, that since I could afford it, and didn't, it meant that I didn't like myself. Well, I started feeling guilty buying the cheap things that I liked and had to remind myself that it was okay. I really do prefer a strange little box of stark-white Chinese face powder or some incredible opera-mask paper cuts for 75 cents.

I had a salesman take two old vases out of a locked case. They had such beautiful hand-painted flowers and insects, and the glaze had that wonderful patina only really old things get. I thought the tag said 800 Hong Kong dollars (about $140), so I felt like I would be nice to myself and get them. In the light the tag said $8000. I didn't buy them. Our life is so spread out and so mobile. I can't take my beautiful possessions with me and it breaks my heart when a cleaning person drops something I've loved. Francis was really sad when he noticed his Art Deco tray was broken by the house-sitter while we were away this last trip.

Great things go to museums. I figure I can see the wonderful public collections of the finest examples of whatever I am interested in at the moment, and it is all dusted and well lit and properly cared for. A lot of things I like are inexpensive and replaceable.

July 25, Pagsanjan

The main road is filled with jeepneys, three-wheeled motorcycles, trucks, bicycles, carts, scooters, dust and smoke. Our house is on a side street. Only an occasional car passes. Lots of kids play out front. Ducks and chickens wander about and the lady across the street walks her pig every morning. Nipa huts made of straw mats with thatched roofs surround us. People lean out of their sliding shuttered windows and chat with each other. I can hear about four radios, a couple of old women sort of squawking by the laundry faucet and a rooster crowing close by. There is wonderful foliage, coconut and banana palms, ferns, bougainvillea, hibiscus, lots of vines and plants with exotic-looking flowers I've never seen before.

Our house is fancy by local standards. It is concrete block with indoor plumbing. We have ceiling fans and round fluorescent lights that make us look blue at night. There is a five-foot statue of the Virgin of Guadalupe in a niche on the staircase. She has glass eyes with real-hair eyelashes. She looks down over the living and dining room. The owner of our house moved into a large nipa hut with a tin roof in the backyard. He is wealthy, his daughter owns the local hotel. He built this house two years ago, but his wife preferred to still cook outside, and, in the hot season, they slept in a thatched hut in the backyard, so they seem quite happy to rent to us. The great-grandmother lives in what was the old summer sleeping hut. She walks bent nearly double, from years of leaning over the laundry trough and bending down in the garden. She still tends the peanuts, beans, eggplant and squash growing in the backyard, and I see her carrying big pails of laundry to the line. The family is very nice to us. They have a son who lives in Florida with his red-haired, Irish wife and three children. The landlord rocks Sofia on his lap and is teaching her to say "Good morning, Grandpa" in Tagalog.

On the plane, I started reading *The Diary of Anaïs Nin*, *1947–1955*, volume 5. A number of women I respect have told me how terrific the diaries are. I almost never read. I have stopped being embarrassed about it only recently. I hardly ever watch television. I am not sure exactly how I get my information. It seems to come into my life in other ways. Someone else may be at home in their living room, watching a TV program about emerging nations. I am here. I don't see it as better or worse. One of the things that fascinated me in the part of Anaïs Nin's diary that I read was her description of some events in 1948 that perfectly fit my experience years later. Odd little things, like her description of meeting Kenneth Anger, or the chickens outside her window in Acapulco. She says of Mexico, "Freedom from the past comes from associating with unfamiliar objects; none of them possesses any evocative power." I feel that freedom here.

July 28, Pagsanjan

We were driving in the car to see the French plantation set. Dean was talking about insects. He said he had read somewhere that the insect population of the world weighs twelve times as much as the human population, and that insects are amazingly adaptable. In relatively few generations, they are able to overcome any poison man invents. So far we have not eliminated one single type of insect. He said that cockroaches have been on the planet for about 4 million years and they haven't changed for the last 350,000.

They're a perfect design, I guess.

July 29, Pagsanjan

This afternoon there wasn't anything I wanted to shoot. Gio and Roman wanted to take the bonca trip up the rapids, so I decided to go along. At the last minute, Martin Sheen's kids went, too. I was put in a boat with his twelve-year-old son. We were riding along, talking about the difference between the rides at Disneyland and Magic Mountain, about bats and spiders and the Olympic Games. He told me he had been in Rome recently, while his father did a picture. He said Ava Gardner was about his best friend. She wouldn't give her address to anybody, but she gave it to him. He said she was really a nice lady, but she was always putting herself down. The whole time we were passing exotic scenery. The river narrowed to a deep gorge with walls so high only a thin strip of sky could be seen at the top. The sheer rock walls were green with moss and ferns. It was damp and cool in the shadows. I could see the details with an exceptional clarity. I thought perhaps it was because my companion wasn't a grown-up talking about how beautiful it was.

The boat bearers shoved and lifted our bonca up the rapids, jumping from rock to rock. They grunted commands in Tagalog as they strained through difficult places. It took over an hour to get up to the main waterfall. There was a raft ride that went behind the waterfall into a cave. It looked fairly dangerous. The little bamboo raft had no sides and the water was churning around the falls. I thought about being responsible if one of the kids fell off. I decided to go. We got totally drenched. On the way back, my boating partner said it was much better and scarier than any of the rides at Disneyland, and it lasted longer.

As we returned downriver our bonca lagged behind the others. I was thinking about Disneyland and about moviemaking. Disneyland doesn't discriminate between the real and the illusion. Real tropical plants surround the plastic motorized hippos in the jungle ride. It is all there, our dream world and our waking world together. Most of the time we are in a duality.

July 31, Pagsanjan

We enrolled Sofia in a school in the next town. They teach in English in the morning and Chinese in the afternoon. She is the first American student who has ever come to the school. The old Chinese director came out and bowed several times and smiled his pleasure at our honoring his school with our child. A Filipina woman translated for him. She said it was his wish that we pay no tuition. Sofia was taken to a first-grade classroom. (The kindergarten was taught only in Tagalog.) All the children were six or seven. She is five. She was taller than most of them. Her blond hair stuck out above the sea of brown faces. The room was bare, except for a blackboard in front and rows of plain wooden desks. The children were crowded two or three to a desk. The teacher seemed very kindly. She placed Sofia in the middle of the second row. The slatted windows were open and strips of light fell on the children wiggling on the hard benches. Sofia was given a notebook and pencil, and the teacher helped her begin copying the phrases from the board. "Come, baby, come," "Come to Mother," "Come to Father." The children were smiling and wiggling as they printed and chanted the phrases over and over again.

The classrooms were around a courtyard that was empty except for a flagpole and a refreshment stand, where the children bought little sandwiches, soft drinks and candy at the one fifteen-minute recess of the morning. School started at 7:20, with flag raising and singing the national anthem, followed by ten minutes of exercises that were half Western military and half Chinese Tai Chi. A man teacher led the student body while a little record player blared out a lively march. There were five or six older girls with badges who went among the younger children to help them with the exercises. Three helpers crowded around Sofia. As they finished, the children formed neat little lines and filed into the classrooms.

Part of me was shocked at leaving my child there as they fitted her with a blue and white uniform and took her to a hard little desk. It was a long way from the Creative Living and Learning Center in San Francisco. But the children looked happy and the teachers were very sweet and jolly. As we left, a little girl had her arm around Sofia, trying to tell her something in Tagalog with an occasional English word mixed in. Francis said it would be a terrific experience for her. It reminded him of Cuba.

Sofia came home for lunch with her book bag and a green reader. The book was about a family with three children and Chonggo, their pet monkey. The mother wore a long, Asian-style dress. I read the last two pages:

God heard Tony and Nita pray,
God heard Mother and Baby pray,
God heard Father pray,
Soon Father was well,
Soon he could get up,

98

Soon he could stand and walk,
Mother, Tony and Nita
Were happy again.
Father was very happy again,
Too.

Let us go to church,
Said Father.
Let us thank God
For making me well.
So Father, Mother, Nita, Tony
And Baby went to church.
They went to church to pray.
They went to church
To thank God for making Father
Well again.

I hadn't expected that to be the reader at the Chinese school.

August 2, Pagsanjan

Last night Vittorio and his family came to dinner. Tonia made pasta. The kitchen was so hot, even with the fan going, she had beads of sweat on her upper lip and her forehead and little rivulets running down her neck. The children were being irritable with each other, so Vittorio took them all out on the front porch to play a game. The idea was to scoot a bottle cap along the flat banister as far as one could without it falling off. A sort of race with each child taking turns. Of course, the caps would fall on the ground continually, and Vittorio would look for them in the bushes with a flashlight. I was amazed at his patience.

Francis, Dean and Fred were sitting on the couch reading some fairly recent newspapers that had come from Manila. I didn't want to help with the cooking. Tonia, Robin and Ester had done everything. I didn't want to help find bottle caps with Vittorio and the kids. I didn't feel that I could just sit down and read newspapers with the men. Some part of me, conditioned to be a proper hostess, kept nagging uncomfortably. Eventually, the pasta was served and we all sat down. The kids fussed about who sat by whom. Fabrizio and Giovanni wanted to sit by Roman, Sofia wanted to sit by Giovanni, Gio didn't want to sit at the corner, Francesca wanted to sit in my place by Francis. I was saying, "Cut it out," to my kids; I don't know what Vittorio was saying in Italian to his. Finally he picked Sofia, crying, out of her chair and put her next to Giovanni, Roman sat by Fabrizio and we more or less got settled. There wasn't quite enough sauce for the spaghetti. Several of the kids complained.

After the pasta, we had a green salad made from the local lettuce. It tastes so much better than the imported iceberg lettuce they serve at the hotel. Tonia began talking about how we should use boiled water to wash all our vegetables. A loudspeaker truck had passed through town warning that there is cholera in the area.

After dinner we sat on the couch and finished the wine. I asked Vittorio how he felt about the first day of shooting at the new location, tomorrow. He said it was almost like beginning a new film; Baler seemed like a completed war and now Part II was beginning. He asked me how my film was going. He said how much he would like to see it, because there was such a fantastic story about the making of *Apocalypse Now*. I had a deep pang of panic. I tried to tell him that I had decided to stop making it the way I was, as an objective documentary, and switch to a subjective personal view that I didn't have a real fix on yet. I could see by his expression that he didn't understand what I was saying, something about the English words I used didn't communicate the idea to him.

I had lots of dreams last night. Francis was restless, too. Several times in the night I got up to put the sheet back on the bed or close the door that had blown open. I could hear the steady rain above the noise of the air conditioner. This morning I was tired at breakfast. I was telling Francis about my fears of going ahead with a straight documentary film because I am not a professional, at best it would be only passable, and that if I changed to make a personal view, maybe no one would be interested in it and feel cheated. And then, how could I integrate what I have already shot objectively, into a personal view? So much money has already been spent that I can't quit. I can't quit, and I don't see clearly how to go on. I was feeling miserable and scared. Francis started laughing. I realized that it was just exactly what *he* had told *me* a few weeks ago. He couldn't go on making the original John Milius script because it didn't really express his ideas, and he couldn't stop because so much money had been spent. People were saying how anxious they were to see the film because it is such an extraordinary story. He didn't know how to turn the film into his personal vision, or if anybody would even be interested in it. He was really scared and miserable, and at just that moment the typhoon came along and gave him the excuse to stop and try to resolve his conflict. He has done a lot of rewriting and torturous struggling with himself, twenty-four hours a day over the last weeks, and has sort of turned a corner inside somewhere. Now most of his fear is focused on how to resolve the ending. He is fairly clear about the journey toward the end and seems ready to shoot today's scene.

I don't see any typhoons ahead for me. I don't know what I'm going to do. Maybe I'll just start from here. I'll set the camera up by my window. It's beginning to rain. Little streams of water are starting to run off the corrugated tin roof of the landlord's hut in the backyard. I can see an old man in a wide straw hat. He is squatting on the path, cutting banana leaves with his bolo knife and making little tents to put over the tiny new plants in the garden so they won't get damaged by a downpour.

August 3, Pagsanjan

Yesterday I didn't go to the set. It was the first day of new shooting. I knew Francis would be tense. The scene was in the interior of the Saigon Hotel with Marty. The set was small and cramped and hot with the lights and humidity. I stayed home and looked out the window and tried to release my fears about what to do next regarding the documentary. I had Doug show me how to load the camera magazines. I had always let others do it. I loaded magazines by myself, sitting on the toilet in Sofia's bathroom in the dark. I realized how simple it was and how mysterious I had allowed it to be.

I am angry at the camera because it does not see as my eyes see. I must first isolate what I want to shoot and then translate every subtlety into camera language. For me there is this frustration between what I see and what the camera records. Vittorio can speak camera language and can see the way a camera sees. I am a chauvinist; I want the camera to see as I do. Vittorio makes another reality with the camera that is not the one that is there. I have seen the one that is there, and it is substantially different. All I want to do is record what is there. I have been used to taking whatever the camera spit out. If I took enough still photos, I always got a few good ones, or I shot it again. That doesn't work for documentary filmmaking. I can't come back the next day, the moment has passed, it was a moving point in time and space that doesn't exist again.

August 4, Pagsanjan

Francis said he had a dream a few nights ago about being on the set of the Saigon Hotel room with Marty and a Green Beret adviser. In the dream, the Green Beret was telling Francis that what he was doing with Marty was wrong, it would never be like that. The Green Beret said those guys were vain, the guy would look in the mirror and admire his beautiful hair and his beautiful mouth. In Francis's dream, he had Marty go to the mirror and look at himself, admire his mouth, etc., and when he turned around, Francis could see that Marty had suddenly turned into Willard.

Yesterday Francis shot the scene in the hotel room. He let Marty get a little drunk, as the character is really supposed to be. He and Marty both knew they were taking a chance. The first layer of the character Marty played was the mystic, the saint, the Christlike version of Willard. Francis pushed him with a few words and he became the theatrical performer, Willard as the Shakespearean actor. Francis prodded him again and he moved to a street tough, a feisty street fighter who has been at the bottom, but is smart, knows some judo, is used to a scrap. At this point, Francis asked him to go to the mirror and look at himself and admire his beautiful hair, his mouth. Marty began this incredible scene. He hit the mirror with his fist. Maybe he didn't mean to. Perhaps he overshot a judo stance. His hand started bleeding. Francis said his impulse was to cut the scene and call the nurse, but Marty was doing the scene. He had gotten to the place where some part of him and Willard had merged. Francis had a moment of not wanting to be a vampire, sucking Marty's blood for the camera, and not wanting to turn off the camera when Marty was Willard. He left it running. He talked Marty through the scene. Two cameras were going.

I was outside in the street, shooting. When I went back to the set, Enrico, Vittorio and the people who had been inside during the scene were coming out, visibly shaken. Silent and disturbed, emotionally affected by the power of Marty/Willard baring his guts in the room.

I waited for Francis to come outside after the wrap. He never came. Finally, I went into the set. Francis and Marty were alone. Marty was lying on the bed, really drunk, talking about love and God. He was singing an old hymn called "Amazing Grace" and trying to get Francis and me to sing with him, holding our hands and crying. He was strong and wiry like a boxer. Francis was trying to be with him and see that he didn't hurt himself. His cut finger had been bandaged. It started to bleed again because he was squeezing our hands, hard, and sometimes hitting edges of the bed. The nurse came in and I helped hold his arm, so she could put a fresh dressing on the cut and try to stop the bleeding. The cut was not deep, but it was right on the knuckle and he kept bending it. Marty asked the nurse to pray and sing and I could see she was praying dead seriously. I thought I should go home and get some espresso coffee in a thermos, but when I started to get up, Marty would take my hand and I couldn't leave.

Janet came with their oldest son and Gray. Marty wanted us to hold hands and pray and confess our fears. There was that stiffness that exists when someone is drunk or on dope and you're not. They're in a different space, you can't get comfortable in theirs or yours. Marty was preaching and carrying on, singing. Everyone was trying to sort of ease him toward the car. The Filipina nurse was praying out loud and saying, "Jesus loves you, Marty." It took about two hours to get him in the car and back to the hotel in the rain.

This morning on the set, the scene called for Marty to have a hangover the morning after in the hotel. When I left, Francis and Marty were talking about yesterday's scene, what had happened and what it meant for the film. It showed a side of Willard that would underlie everything else he did. It showed his insides to the audience, to Marty and to the other actors. One of the main problems of the character as it had originally been written was that Willard was always the observer looking on, and you didn't really know who he was, what he was like. Maybe that is why different actors turned down the part. Francis wanted an actor to have confidence in him, even if it wasn't all written in the script. Confidence that he would find a way to get to that moment where the actor, the person and the character merged into reality when the cameras are rolling.

Later, we talked about whether the scene would have as much power on the screen as it had for everyone on the set during shooting. The room had been charged with the possibility that Marty might lunge at the camera or attack Francis. There was that emotional electricity in the room, anything could happen. They were inside somebody, in his personal territory, with a man alone in his most private moment.

August 7, Pagsanjan

Sofia is out in the street in front of the house in her shorts and bare feet, chasing the little kids who have gathered at the corner. It started when she went out in the rain in her shiny red raincoat and some kids came to look at her. She began putting on a show for them, pouring cups of rain-water on her head. When the rain stopped, she continued. She played she was Jaws and chased one kid or another while they tried to get away, and the rest screamed and laughed. People are leaning out of their windows and grown-ups have gathered. The children call "Sofia!" and try to get her to chase them. I wonder what being the center of all the attention is doing to her.

At school the children come from all the grades to look at her, call her name, hold her hand and touch her. Sofia has started going to school in the afternoon now. She is in the Chinese kindergarten. The first day the adjustment period was the reverse of the American idea where the child slowly gets used to a strange new environment. When she entered the room, the teacher stood her up in front of the class and taught her to say, "Good afternoon, classmates," in Chinese. They all shouted, "Good afternoon, Sofia," then the teacher had her write the Chinese character for "people" on the board. They seemed to acknowledge the fact that all the children wanted to look at Sofia, and they just put her right up there in front, immediately, and got it over with. We would be doing such a child psychology dance to prevent the kid from being traumatized. Maybe it is actually less of a trauma just to tell the truth. Look, kid, you look different to us, we'd all like to have a good look at you. And just do it. Sofia seemed glad to have something specific to do. She went to the board and tried to draw the character as best she could. When she finished, she had to repeat the word. The teacher asked her to say it louder, so she did, and all the kids clapped and she went to her seat. Sofia was part of the class.

August 8, Pagsanjan

Last evening was the first night shooting. It was at the Do
Long Bridge set. We had all been there several times during
the day, but something happened at night. Maybe it was
the fires that special effects started, and the arc lights illu-
minating the hundreds of extras in costume in the
trenches. Maybe it was knowing that after all the rehearsing and preparing, this was it. There was a kind of electricity in the air. Parts seemed like a circus. There were so
many trucks and strings of lights and cables and people
going in and out of the darkness as if the show were about
to begin. The main event. The set looked extraordinary. It
was better than anyone had imagined. Most things seemed
to fall short of expectations, but this was somehow more
than anyone had anticipated. It was very hot and humid. I
could see the sweat running down people's faces when they
passed in front of a light. Both channels of the radio were
going as the first shot was being set up. I could hear, "We
need ten Vietnamese extras to be dead in the water. Light
the downstream burners. Makeup check for GI extras now.
Bring in the crane to the upstream position on the tropical
side. Bring the generator barge to the camera first position," on and on. A light rain began to fall. I was under
some coconut palms by a wall of sandbags on the ridge. I
couldn't feel the rain, but I could see it in the paths of light.
There were millions of insects around the big lights in the
towers. The electricians had wrapped T-shirts around their
heads. Only Luciano was just in his bathing suit with a tool
belt and gloves. He shouted over the megaphone in Italian
to the other light towers and across the river to the generator operator and electricians on that side. I could smell
the exhaust from the generator truck near us.

A coconut fell into the trench just in front of me. A GI
extra leaped up and grabbed for his helmet. There was a lot

of laughing about how he almost got killed, on his way to stardom, by a falling coconut. Several guys tossed it around like a football. The waiting went on. All the extras had live blanks in their machine guns and rifles, and they were excited about firing them. Several swimmers were in the river rehearsing laying mines and dragging dead Vietnamese out of the water. People were drinking sodas or smoking, sitting quietly in the dark, waiting for the camera barge and the PBR to get into position upstream for the first rehearsal of all the action. Occasionally special effects would fire a test rocket or a flare and the whole set would be illuminated. I could see all the extras silhouetted in the trenches and the cables and technicians and trucks in the background. Giant fingers of lightning flashed in the sky above the bridge. It was a kind of tropical lightning that none of us had seen before. I could hear the special effects men laughing over the radio, saying, "Gee, that one was great, Joe, what did you use to do that?"

Finally there was a dinner break and everyone moved toward the road and back to where the caterers had set up. There was a palm frond roof over a large area and rows and rows of tables with lines of crews and cast snaking past the buffet tables. The people who lived in the nipa huts along the road stood around the edge of the eating area, watching the technicians and GIs and everyone having dinner. Little kids called out, "Hi, Joe," choruses of little voices. The site of the set was where a bridge had been blown up by the Japanese in World War II, and never rebuilt. The concrete footings, sticking up from the riverbed, formed the base for the bridge our crew built. The set bridge is scheduled to be blown up, too.

Gio was an extra. He had a full pack GI outfit on and was carrying an M-16 automatic rifle. He had black makeup on his face. He is twelve. He was as tall as some of the shorter men. After the meal break, everyone got into position and the rehearsals began. The first shot got off about 11:00 P.M., with the PBR coming downriver and the camera boat trying to maintain a position behind and to the side. Flares, rockets and several big flame balls were set off. It looked great from where I was shooting. While they set up for the second take, it started to rain again. Roman had fallen asleep on some sandbags, and the company nurse told me I should take him home, he would get sick. I woke him up, but he didn't want to go until after the next take. One of the extras gave him a flak jacket to put on the ground next to the wall where it was relatively dry and he went back to sleep. The second shot didn't go until about 12:30 A.M. I woke Roman up, but he kept closing his eyes and missed most of the main effects. I gave the camera to Doug to see if he could get some shots of the effects men during the next take, and I started home with Roman. As we walked along the road toward the car, I could see in the windows of the nipa huts, lit by the production lights. People were sleeping on the floor under mosquito netting or wrapped in a cloth. Francis and Gio came home at around 3:00 A.M.

August 12, Pagsanjan

Catholicism seems decorative here. There are Madonnas and crucifixes, and the jeepneys have religious pictures on their dashboards, but there isn't a heavy Catholic overtone to everything like in Mexico. The Pagsanjan Family Planning Clinic is right across the street from the main church. Sofia is very interested in the story of Jesus. When we got out of the shower the other morning, she wrapped up in her towel and told me she was Baby Jesus. She wanted me to put my towel over my head and play Mother Mary.

August 13, Pagsanjan

It gets dark between six thirty and seven. The evening here is one of my favorite times of the day. People put on their one electric light or kerosene lantern, and as you walk by an open window or door, it is like a framed painting of a little scene. People don't seem to use curtains, or when they do, they are tied in a knot to let in any little current of air. In the daytime, the interiors of the houses are dark, as everyone seeks the cool shadows, but at night, the windows are like illuminated tableaus.

We have all our windows open, too, although we have the luxury of screens. Often, in the evening we look up from the dinner table and there are people chatting at our corner and looking in at us. We are like the local television for our block.

August 14, Pagsanjan

I am at Vittorio's house. Francesca is making zeppole in the kitchen, trying to teach the Filipina maid how to cook them in the hot oil. The maid is getting splattered and wants Francesca to make the globs of dough smaller. Neither can understand the other's few words of English. At the table in the dining room, Tonia, Luciano and his wife are talking loudly, animatedly in Italian. I just get an occasional word like *bambino*. I think they are arguing about the care of Luciano's adopted baby. On the screened porch, Francis and Vittorio are discussing what to do about the scene in the trench that shoots in a few hours. I have taken a couple of stills in the kitchen of the sink and the dish drainer, backlit from the windows that look into the garden. But, essentially, I am stuck. I don't want to sit down with Francis and Vittorio in the middle of their conversation. It's too hot in the kitchen. I don't want to make Tonia and Luciano feel uncomfortable by sitting down near them. She has already said "Excuse me" several times. I am sort of leaning against the wall here, trying to look comfortably occupied, writing in my notebook.

Last night the mood on the set was different. It was the sixth consecutive night of shooting at Do Long Bridge. The circus mood was gone. The setup was down in a trench. It had been raining and the bottom of the trench was full of water. The shot called for a dolly track. I watched Alfredo work. His men shoveled in a lot of sand and stomped and packed it until the water disappeared into a mass of mud. They laid a layer of sandbags and placed two-by-twelves on top of that. The wood was wet from the rain, and really heavy. I could see the sweat spraying off the men as they moved in front of the lights. When the bottom of the trench was solid, Alfredo laid the track and leveled it with wooden wedges. The dolly was lifted onto the track, the mount and the camera were set. One man had a pole with a chamois attached to the end, and he leaned into the trench and cleaned the mud off the track each time the dolly passed.

Francis began to rehearse the shot with the actors and the camera. On about the third rehearsal, a large section of the trench wall caved in, covering the track with a couple of tons of dirt and sandbags. It was a long time before it was cleared and they were ready to shoot. The shot called for smoke. The special effects man turned on his spray canister, and laid in a blanket of gray mist. It smelled like oily insect repellent. The wind kept changing, and for each take they put in a new batch. Marty, Sam and the camera crew were coughing and rubbing their eyes. I got back a ways. From where I was, it looked beautiful, with the smoke all backlit, the strings of lights on the bridge and the rockets.

Later in the evening, they needed a flare up in the air at a certain height. A Filipino shimmied up a coconut palm. He went up about eighty feet and attached a pulley so the effects man could hoist a flare up and get it down to reload between takes. The night went very slowly with several setups in the trench, each requiring effects. I left around 3:00 A.M. Francis got home about 6:00 this morning.

August 18, Pagsanjan

I was sitting on top of a pile of sandbags on the ridge, watching the evening fall at the Do Long Bridge set. The strings of lights on the bridge came on. They looked like the kind they use at Italian street *festas* in New York City. Luciano's men were up in the lighting towers getting ready to turn on the arcs. I was watching an electrician cut a round yellow gel for a light near me. All the departments were just getting going. The first shot was on the PBR at the river's edge. The camera was already on the boat and Francis was down there talking to Vittorio. The evening looked pretty with the reflections on the water and the special effects fires starting up along the banks. I went down to the boat and got on just as they were pulling out. The first moment reminded me of a night boat ride somewhere, like the Seine, or maybe the Rhine. It was too dark to see the shore. We headed upriver and there was something festive about being on the water in the night with just the running lights. Then the boat swung around, heading downriver toward the set. The radios started blaring. All the lighting instructions were going out on Vittorio's radio and the special effects men were talking over Jerry's. The boat was idling, trying to stay in position while the camera was being set. The shot was a close-up on Albert Hall.

There was a long discussion about whether Albert's look was supposed to be to camera right or camera left. The script supervisor was sure it was camera right, but Vittorio thought it was camera left and wanted to shoot it both ways to be sure. Jerry said there wasn't time to do both. The exhaust smoke from the diesel engines was blowing on us. The evening began to look like just hard work.

August 20, Pagsanjan

It is 3:15 A.M. I have just come home from the set. It was supposed to be the last night of shooting. at Do Long Bridge. But it went very slowly. A day of delay means $30,000–$50,000. This set has fallen behind two days. There are many grumbles about why. There are a lot of reasons. Sometimes the camera setup seems slow, sometimes the special effects seem to take a long time to reload. Sometimes an actor needs more rehearsal. Sometimes Francis adds some new dialogue. Tonight Francis laid out a shot early in the evening and came home for about forty minutes to have a cup of soup while the lighting and dolly track were being set. It rained all the time he was home. When he got back to the location, the river had risen nearly six feet. The scene was to be played with the actor walking along the bank through the mud to the boat. Now there was no bank, the scene had to be played with the guy wading waist-deep in the water. Everything was slowed down; by midnight spirits were sagging as it became apparent that the evening's work was going to take another night.

August 23, Pagsanjan

This morning we got up early. I was really tired. I stood at the sink running the cold water on my hand, waiting for it to get warm to wash my face. I stood there a long time before I remembered that there is no hot water. Francis had to be on the set at 7:00 A.M. and it is a fair drive from the house. He was doing a rehearsal with all the actors at the table of the French plantation. Gio and Roman are in the scene, too, so they had to go at the same time. We hadn't eaten breakfast, but we got in the car and I brought some hard-boiled eggs and some tangerines. Roman was leaning on me, putting on his shoes as we drove, and I realized he hadn't brushed his teeth or combed his hair.

I am the mother of these children, the wife of the director of this multimillion-dollar production, and I hadn't given a thought to my family this morning. I had only been thinking about reloading my still camera with some fast film to photograph the interior of the set before the people and lighting equipment were in the way. Riding along in the car I began going through my wife/mother versus artist argument in my head for about the five hundredth time. Both sides have this perfectly reasonable position; neither gives in.

Over the years, Francis has continually been frustrated with me. I have a closet full of equipment at home. He bought me an animation stand when I was making little animated films, a jigsaw when I was making plastic sculpture. I have a sewing machine from my fabric collage period, an airbrush I used for a series of drawings, a Nikon for still photography. I go through each phase arguing with myself the whole way. Saying, "Why am I doing this? I should be focusing on the children and Francis, they are more important than my projects." Yet, I am always compelled by my current interest, wanting to explore it but never getting it to blend comfortably with my family.

When we got to the set I could see that Francis was irritated; there were already people pounding nails and fussing around. He likes to get there before anybody and have that moment of complete stillness to think about the staging before all the other considerations creep in. He asked everyone to leave the room, but that wasn't the same as coming to a perfectly empty, silent set. It makes him feel like he is appearing to be the temperamental director, chasing them out.

I took some shots downstairs and then, as the actors arrived and the rehearsal began, I went upstairs to see if the bedroom was dressed yet. Bob was working on it, just placing the last few things.

I told him the rooms were a work of art. He said, "Thank you," almost before I finished, as if he meant, "Well, of course." He told me about this odd forties dresser he had found by the side of the road and how he had had it painted with scenes from French fairy tales on the cream-colored background. He said that he had really wanted to cover the dresser with leather and trim it with brass but he knew that Francis would get mad if he spent the money to do it.

He was placing some old photos on the bedside table that were supposed to be the actress's relatives. He told me that they were actually photos of his mother and grandmother, and some of the photos of children were he and his brother. The photo stuck in the mirror of the dresser was of his aunt, and downstairs, over the piano, was his mother and father's wedding picture. His life and his art were all mixed together. Why am I always struggling to get them to blend? Francis gets them together, too. He is downstairs right now rehearsing a scene in which Roman plays a child at the dinner table asked to recite a poem by his father. That is right from our own dining room. Francis has asked Roman to recite that French poem at our table, dozens of times.

August 24, Pagsanjan

Today I shot some footage of the construction at the main set, Kurtz Compound. It is supposed to be a decaying Cambodian temple on the river. Dean's department is building a huge temple and a number of outlying buildings out of adobe blocks. I could hear the pumps pumping water from the river up to the area where the adobe was being made. There were crews of men moving the dried blocks. Each block weighed three hundred pounds. Four men would shoulder a bamboo sling and carry a block to one of the building sites. Bamboo hoists, with a long line of men pulling on thick ropes, lifted the blocks into place. Barges ferried men and materials across the river to the work on the other side. I was amazed at how primitive the construction methods were. John La Sandra told me that manpower costs less than machine power here. He said it was more efficient to explain what he wanted built and then let it be done in the local way. He told me that there were nearly seven hundred laborers all together, with all the wood-carvers, mold makers, carpenters, etc.

Coconut palms were being cleared where bamboo huts will be constructed for the Indians who are being recruited to live on the set. In the script, Kurtz's band of renegade soldiers has trained a tribe of local Montagnard Indians to be a fighting team. They live in huts by the temple. Rather than dress up Filipino extras every day, Francis asked Eva, a production assistant, to go to a northern province where the rice terraces are and recruit a real tribe of primitive people to come live on the set and be in the scenes. I hear she is trying to make a contract with a group of 250 Ifugao Indians. The contract includes food, salary, medical care and a number of chickens, pigs and carabao for sacrificial purposes.

August 25, Pagsanjan

Alfredo came at 1:00 P.M. to take us to his house for Sunday dinner. We had just gotten up and were having coffee in our robes. We had gone to bed about four in the morning. Francis had forgotten about the invitation. We dressed quickly and got the kids to comb their hair and we went to the Italian's house. Alfredo's Neapolitan wife was there and his brother, Mario, and his wife, their twenty-two-year-old daughter and a tiny grandchild who looked totally white with blue eyes and yellow-white hair in the arms of a Filipina maid.

We sat down to a meal of pasta with a sauce of olive oil, anchovies, black olives, tomatoes, capers, tuna and garlic. It was super, but I am used to starting the day with a scrambled egg. They kept telling me to eat more. I am apparently too thin for their taste, "too small for such a big husband" was what I could make in translation of their conversation, all in Italian. It was really an effort to eat enough pasta to satisfy them. By the time they took the plates away, I was uncomfortably stuffed. Then they served roast chicken with rosemary and browned potatoes. I had forgotten all about the possibility that there could be more. After the chicken, there was a huge platter of shrimp, then little artichokes in olive oil that had been brought from Italy. Salad was served and then bread and cheese. The whole time they were saying, "What's the matter, you don't like Italian food? You hardly eat. A bird eats more."

When the coffee was served, I took some pictures of everyone at the table. They all turned toward the camera and posed. There was something about the flowered green, plastic tablecloth, the paper napkins in a glass and the women in cotton sundresses, with slip straps showing, that seemed totally Italian, with no overlay of the Philippines at all.

I walked out into the garden and there were several ladies' cotton undershirts on the clothesline. I wondered when they wore those in this heat. The Italian crew on the production are amazing about their personal decorum. Shooting in some muddy trench in the middle of the night, there Vittorio will be with his starched linen shirt, opened halfway to the waist, exposing his tan chest and thick gold Gucci chain. The Americans wear cutoff jeans and stained T-shirts. On one incredibly hot day, in a sweaty patch of jungle, I got a little piece of ice from the soft drink chest to rub on my face and I let the water drip down my shirt. Luciano walked by with a silk scarf tied around his neck, looking really dashing.

When we got back to our house, the French actors were there, waiting to have Sunday dinner with us.

August 26, Pagsanjan

I was talking to Christian Marquand. He said, "Have you seen the big set? It is an incredible construction. It is the best sculpture I have ever seen. It is outside, you can walk all around, there is sky and earth. It is all there for two months and then gone. It is like an exhibition, but somehow better."

Maybe it was his French accent that separated out the information in some new way so I could hear it. All my life I have wanted to be at the center of the really current, pertinent art scene. Be there when it is happening, and know and really be friends with the artists, like when you read about so-and-so, who used to play chess with Duchamp, or drink beer with Jackson Pollock or something. At times I have followed the art world. Met various artists, like Oldenburg, Christo, Andy Warhol, Poons, etc., but they were already famous and established. It was after the fact. I just felt my same shy, uncomfortable self, like with any people I don't know well. I have looked for the center of the art scene. I went to Paris as a student. I lived in Venice, California. When I looked for the art scene around 1970, I thought it was in New York. I saw minimal art end and conceptual art come into the spotlight. I agreed with the conceptual art tenet that pertinent art of the mid-seventies was not the making of a timeless art object, but about creating an event in time and space. But the conceptual art events I went to were mostly dumb and boring. Contemporary dance seemed more alive. I kept thinking the "real" art must be going on somewhere else, maybe Milano or Documenta or some exotic place. I never felt like I was really where it was at. I know Francis has felt that same thing, wanting to be part of where it really was happening. He has always wanted to be in this wonderful community of artists at the moment that people would talk about later as some golden era. He tried to make it happen in San Francisco. He dreamed of this group of poets, film-makers and writers who would drink espresso in North Beach and talk of their work, and it would be good. They would publish their writing in *City* magazine, do new plays at the Little Fox Theatre, make experimental films at American Zoetrope. There would be this terrific center of exciting art. He spent a lot of money and energy trying to make it happen. When it didn't, he got angry and frustrated and maybe, mostly sad. He threw his Oscars out the window and left for the Philippines.

Well, just this morning, I realized that this is *it!* Right here in Pagsanjan, of all places. I couldn't see it because it isn't some North Beach café or picturesque studio in Paris or a New York City loft. It's right here. Here we both are, right here where we dreamed of being. I started to laugh. When you stop looking for something, you see it right in front of you. This is that community of artists. It's Dean, Bob, Vittorio, Enrico, Joe, Marty and Alfredo. When I think about it, I really believe that this film is about the most pertinent artwork going on today. We call what Dean is doing, sets; that's an old label. He is probably making the most interesting art sculpture event going on anywhere in the world right now. Vittorio is a world-class visual artist. A poet with light. Francis is writing, only he is not in a romantic-looking garret, he is bent over his electric type-writer right here, sweating in Pagsanjan, so he doesn't see it. Francis is actually the conceptual artist, the ultimate conceptual artist I have been wanting to know. The most right-on artist of 1976. This is that moment we've dreamed of being present at. We're swatting mosquitoes, and eating mangos, it doesn't look like it's supposed to, but I'll bet this is that point in time somebody will label as *it*. I am still laughing.

August 27, Pagsanjan

Coming up in the car this morning to the French plantation set, Francis was talking about the scene at the table
yesterday and what went wrong. He had the actors do the
whole scene in one long piece, over and over, trying to get
a sense of the experience of being at that table as a family,
arguing with each other. Going through an experience together to produce moments of reality that you don't get
when you shoot in pieces, two lines at a time. But it didn't
work. Francis was really frustrated, because that technique
of creating an experience has always given him some terrific moments and this time it didn't work. He went over
and over with himself, why? He decided that maybe it was
because they were French, and the English lines were a
barrier, or that some of them weren't professional actors.
He was angry that the set had gone over budget, and he
had tried to save money on casting. He kept saying, "An
audience doesn't give a shit about the authentic antiques
on the set, they care about the people in the scene." Vittorio wanted to break the scene into little pieces and do just
a couple of lines at a time until it worked. That's the way
they do it in Europe. Francis said that when Bobby De
Niro first worked with Bertolucci, he said it drove him crazy
because he never got to develop the character from doing
the whole scene, he had to play it line by short line. The
European approach is to start with the frame, and get each
frame right. Francis works by getting the emotion of the
scene going and asking the camera to capture it. This
morning, Francis is going to try it in short pieces.

August 27, French Plantation Set

Francis is feeling angry and trapped. The art department has made their art without sparing expense. What they have made is extraordinary, but it is so complete and detailed there is no way Francis can get it all on camera. Vittorio is oriented toward getting the most perfectly beautiful composition of light and dark in each frame. Visual painting that is extraordinary, but it takes a long time to get all the elements just right, and time is money. The shooting goes very slowly when each setup is taken to such perfection. When the shooting goes slowly, the actors wind down and Francis loses the momentum that keeps his creative juices going. Francis works best when he doesn't have much time and relies on his intuitive decisions. He works by shooting the scenes long, using the emotion that develops and then whacking out huge hunks in the editing room. If he shoots the scenes long, with Vittorio's standards of perfection, it will take months longer than it is scheduled and run up the budget by millions. Francis is feeling the pressure of being at the financial limit, having all the chips on the table. His deal is such that, as the film goes over budget, he has to guarantee the overages personally. If the film is a blockbuster it will be okay, but if the film is pretty good but has gone far over budget, he could end up being wiped out financially and owe millions. I think about that sometimes. Perhaps there is a part of me that wants him to fail. Be back in some simple life-style and all that. At one point in the past, it was really strong, as if returning to a "simple" life would take me out of where I was and I would be happier. At least I know now that it doesn't change things that much. You can be rich and unhappy, or poor and unhappy. I guess women have a hard time as the man grows more successful, powerful, and wish for a time when the balance was more equal. It comes from the fact that the relationship changes. The successful man is usually good at what he does, and likes it, and spends a lot of time doing it—and less and less time with his wife and family. When I stopped feeling like a victim, I started having a lot of fun with Francis. We have odd moments of really interesting time together, rather than more usual amounts of time half tuned out.

August 30, French Plantation Set

I am sitting in this fancy chair on the French plantation set. It is 8:00 P.M. The day was supposed to end at 6:00; everyone is tired and on edge. The shot is a master of the dinner table. It has to be finished so that the actors can go home tomorrow. Luciano has burned his hand in a hurry to change a light. There is something exciting about a scene finishing, and maybe some kind of resistance to having it end. I look around at all the things on the set that were never in any shot. Rented for nothing. The last shot just finished. The French actors are being sentimental and kissing good-bye. There is a kind of camaraderie that takes place, like closing night of a play. Every day for the last five days they have been together at the dinner table. They started out eating the French dinner with gusto; after five days of the food served, over and over and over again, under the hot lights, it was all they could do to pick at it.

August 31, French Plantation Set

This morning I am sitting in another uncomfortable French chair. Francis is rehearsing Marty and Aurore. There is so much furniture on this set, Francis is bumping into things as he tries to step back to look for the shot through his viewfinder. There are chairs, objects, tables, plant stands, stuff everywhere, four times as much as could be in a real house. It is oppressive to look at it in one way; every inch of wall is heavy with hanging pictures, animal heads, antlers, paintings, mirrors, musical instruments, something everywhere. Every table is a clutter with figurines, books, cigarette boxes, plants, candy dishes, fans, vases, photos. All the furniture is upholstered with a different-patterned fabric, patterned rugs. A creation of instant clutter, a family living in the same place for a hundred years, sitting here it looks awful and wonderful. It will look super in the film. The camera can only take in a portion of what's here. It will make the frame that is photographed look rich. The camera won't pass a square foot of blank wall. Actually, there is something Francis likes about all this stuff. It appeals to his sense of a family, all living in the same place for a long time. During his childhood his family moved about thirty times. I guess he would like our house in San Francisco to feel permanent. He has always been trying to get me to finish furnishing it. I think he means put all the clutter around. All the things from over the years, so it looks like a family lived there permanently instead of off and on the last three years. I am always trying to get rid of the little things and get down to clean, simple design. I would like to be somehow completely at home within myself, able to be anywhere in the world and be complete with just what's in my suitcase. I want to live right where I am, and the truth is, a lot of the days of each year I am not in my own home. I like to leave the past in the past. It is really

124

over for me. When I am not in the present, I am speculating about the future. Francis feeds very strongly on the past. He looks at the present through the past. We are such opposites. The more I see it, the more I marvel at how opposite we are. I spent a lot of years resisting the differences, being angry, making myself right and him wrong. The more I see him as he is, my total opposite, and enjoy with amazement how we are attracted to our polar opposites, the more I love him.

September 2, Pagsanjan

I went to the French plantation set to see how Francis was doing and how the boys were holding up. The shot was down on the dock, so I walked down there and found Francis in the shade talking to a heavyset man with short gray hair. When I got closer, the man said, "Hi, Ellie." He looked familiar and then I realized that he was Marlon Brando. I was fascinated that he recognized me and knew my name after such brief meetings. He seemed to be looking at me in microscopic detail. As if he noticed my eyebrows move slightly, or could see the irregular stitching on the buttonhole of my shirt pocket. Not in a judgmental way, just in a complete absorption of all the details.

Later, Francis was telling me that is part of what makes him such a great actor. He develops a fix, a vision of a character, down to the most minute detail. Francis has a more conceptual vision. He has the overall idea of how he wants the film to be and he counts on Dean and Vittorio and the actors to fill in many of the details.

September 4

I was talking to Jerry. He said that it seems like almost everyone on the production is going through some personal transition, a "journey" in their life. Everyone who has come out here to the Philippines seems to be going through something that is affecting them profoundly, changing their perspective about the world or themselves, while the same thing is supposedly happening to Willard in the course of the film. Something is definitely happening to me and to Francis.

September 4, Pagsanjan

Marlon is very overweight. Francis and he are struggling with how to change the character in the script. Brando wants to camouflage his weight and Francis wants to play him as a man eating all the time and overindulging.

I heard there are some real cadavers in body bags at the Kurtz Compound set. I asked the propman about it; he said, "The script says 'a pile of burning bodies'; it doesn't say a pile of burning dummies."

This morning Francis was talking about the Kurtz set being so big that there seemed to be no way to get it all in

126

the frame. The only way to get it was perhaps to come in close and look at specific portions to give a sense of the whole. In a way, that is the same problem he is facing in the script. The ideas of what Kurtz represents are so big that when you try to get a handle on them they are almost undefinable. He has to define the specifics to give a sense of the whole. The production reflects the same thing. It is so big it only seems to make sense in specific ways. Today I have been thinking that the only way that I can show the enormity of the making of *Apocalypse Now* is by showing the details and hoping they give a sense of the larger picture.

———

Francis came home tonight really excited after his long talk with Marlon. He said that Marlon was really incredible. The greatest actor he has ever met, extremely hardworking. Brando had improvised all day. Going one way, then going another, never quitting. They had toughed it out until they came up with a way to go with his character. Brando was going to do something he had never tried before. He was going to play a bigger-than-life character, a mythical figure, a theatrical personage. He is the master of the natural, realistic performance and he was going to go for a different style of acting for the first time in his career. They haven't quite worked out all the details. It will have to be refined over the next few days, but Francis is really excited and he says Marlon is, too.

September 5, Pagsanjan

Late in the afternoon I was standing on the main steps of
the temple with Francis and Marlon. The two of them were
talking about Kurtz. Francis had asked Marlon to reread
Heart of Darkness. Now Marlon was saying how his character should be more like Kurtz was in the book. Francis
said, "Yes, that's what I've been trying to tell you. Don't
you remember, last spring, before you took the part, when
you read *Heart of Darkness* and we talked?"

Marlon said, "I lied. I never read it."

September 6, Pagsanjan

Dennis Hopper is here. It's the first time I've met him. We
have a connection. I have only given two interviews in my
life where I have really tried to talk about myself as a
woman in relation to Francis. One interview was with
Daria Halprin, the other with Brooke Hayward. Both are
ex-wives of Dennis.

September 7, Pagsanjan

I took the boys to the airport yesterday to send them back to San Francisco and school. Gio gave me an obligatory gotta-hug-Mom-type embrace. Roman was just the opposite, holding on to me, hugging and kissing, starting for the gate, coming back for more hugs and kisses and then rushing through the gate, looking back, going a few steps, waving and looking for the last look. I could feel the crying welling up in me, wanting to just let it all come out and wail in pain at the separation, cry out at life for taking my children from me for their own growth and good and maybe, in some way, for mine. I felt that if I let myself cry, it would be even harder for Roman. Maybe appear to him that he was somehow doing it to me. I didn't want to burden him with that, so I turned away from the gate and there was Sofia saying, "Can we get a Coke now?"

I have been crying here in my room, trying not to make noise because all the windows are open in the heat. I just want to be alone and confront my sadness and get past it. My nose is running and there are black smudges on the Kleenex. The trip to Manila was hot. We had all the windows open and drove through clouds of thick exhaust from the trucks and traffic. We were all feeling a little sick when we got there. On the way back in the evening, there was a picture-postcard sunset framed by the back window of the car. It got dark, and started to rain. Sofia was talking a mile a minute. Now and then she would say, "Right, Mom?" and I'd say, "What's that again?" My mind kept drifting away from her chatter. Finally, I guess I wasn't answering her, so she said, "Are you falling asleep or what?" I told her I was just thinking about how my best friends were far away and I missed them. She said, "You know, Mom, you could pick out a person here and just be nice to them, and share with them and they could be your friend. Isn't that a good idea?"

September 8, Pagsanjan

Francis got up at four this morning and went down to his room to write. About six he came into the bedroom and woke me up. He had just figured out why he hasn't been able to resolve the ending of the script. He has been struggling for over a year now, with different drafts of the end, trying to get it right. He said he just realized that there was no simple solution to the script. Just as there was no simple right answer as to why we were in Vietnam. Every time he tried to take the script one direction or the other, he met up with a fundamental contradiction, because the war was a contradiction. A human being contains contradictions. Only if we admit the truth about ourselves, completely, can we find a balance point between the contradictions, the love and the hate, the peace and the violence which exist within us.

We were talking for a long time and it was getting late, so I got dressed. We had some coffee and rode out to the set. It was eight thirty and Marlon was supposed to be there at eight. The assistant director was saying, "What shall we do? We've never worked with Brando before, shall we send another car for him, or how shall we handle it?" Francis said that Marlon would probably be late the first few days.

It seemed to me that Francis thought Marlon was late because the part was still not clearly defined in his mind. Finally, Marlon came around ten and he and Francis went to sit in his houseboat dressing room to talk it out.

At one in the afternoon, the company wrapped for the day and the cast and crew were sent home. Francis is still talking in there and it's past seven in the evening now.

September 9, Pagsanjan

The Ifugaos came to live on the set and be in the film. Last
Saturday they had a feast. The priests and old men of the
tribe sat in the priests' house and chanted. I wanted to film
the ceremony so their mayor asked permission for me to
shoot. I was told if I entered I could not leave during the
first set of chants, which took over an hour. I climbed up
the steep steps with the camera and two portable lights.
Larry followed with the recorder. Inside, there were about
twenty men, squatting on the floor, around an arrangement
of dry stalks of rice. There was a bowl of rice wine in the
middle, a large ceramic jug of wine stood at one end and a
feather crown on a black slab of wood was at the other end.
The ceremony began with the old priest drinking some of
the wine from the bowl and passing the coconut-shell cup
around. It tasted sort of sweet and fruity, like warm sangria.
It seemed pretty strong. The priest started singing and the
others joined him. The sound was strange. It reminded me
of a film I once saw about primitive tribes of New Guinea.

The men were wearing loincloths. Some had Western-
style sport shirts on top. Others had tribal blankets around
their shoulders. The mayor was sitting near me. He was
educated in Manila and speaks very good English. He told
me that the songs were telling a long legend about a couple
and their life. The story begins with the babies in their
mothers' wombs and tells of their experiences of childhood,
growing up, and meeting and marrying, the events of their
life together, their children, growing rice and passing into
old age. It takes about twelve hours to complete all the
verses. About every fifteen minutes they would complete
four long stanzas and the priest would drink a few swallows
of wine, then continue on. I shot the two loads of film I
had and I sat back on the floor, prepared to endure the
monotony until it was appropriate to leave. As I sat there,

the chanting seemed more and more hypnotic, like a meditation. It was totally soothing, I had no desire to leave. It wasn't the wine either, because I had purposely only tasted it so that I could keep a sharp focus.

At one point the song was saying Coppola, Coppola, Coppola, over and over again. The mayor told me that the song always includes the name of the owner of the house where it is being sung. I lost all sense of linear time and was just there, not trying to make it fit into any pigeonhole of logic or string it together with the rest of the events in my life. So many nonreasonable things have happened to me since I have been in the Philippines, I no longer try to make them all fit a reasonable, linear context. I see things, notice them, the way you do in dreams. Here, the waking world and the dream world have many things in common. The line between the two is not abrupt and definitive. It doesn't seem to be for the Ifugaos either. They seem to have a kind of equilibrium all their own.

Some of the men were passing betel nut around in little purses. They were chewing and spitting through the slats in the floor. I could hear the spit hit the mud below. The houses are up on stilts about ten feet off the ground, with pigs and chickens living beneath. Eventually, the old priest stood up and went to the door and down the steep steps. That seemed to be the signal for everyone to file out into the night. Outside, some of the Ifugaos were dancing around a pole to the beat of a cast-iron gong. I watched for a while and then went home.

The next morning I came back with Larry at about 7:00 A.M. The priests had been chanting all night and were still at it. I got a few shots, but nothing much happened until about 10:00 A.M. Then, they all came out and sat down on a mat under the house. It was getting very hot in the sun. I kept trying to find a camera angle I liked that was in the shade. Suddenly, some young Ifugao men grabbed a pig that was rooting near the house. They tied its feet together. The noise of the pig squealing was astounding. They tied up four more and brought them to a clearing about twenty

132

feet in front of the priests. The squealing was so loud you almost couldn't talk above it. The chanting continued, then the oldest priest came out and started dancing around the pigs. He is supposedly in his eighties. He was spritely and graceful. He held out a cup of rice wine and took several sips and then sprinkled it on the largest pig in the course of the dance. Various men came out from under the house and danced with sort of fluttering, birdlike motions around the pigs. Then they would go back and chant a few more verses. Some chickens were brought out in woven cages. The old priest selected one and danced around with it. He placed it on the back of the largest pig. It did not try to fly away. The mayor told me that was a good omen. He said that early in the morning the priest had killed a chicken and looked at its bile. The signs were very positive. The priests were very pleased about that. They said that this group of Ifugaos would be traveling together again, in the future, and that the work they were doing would be seen by many people around the world and make a lot of money.

The dancing and chanting continued for about an hour. The pigs quieted down now and then. It seemed very peaceful at times, with just the steady sound of the chanting coming from under the house, and then an occasional dancer carrying out some aspect of the ritual. Finally, a dancer appeared with a long knife. He pierced the heart of the biggest pig and put a stick into the hole so that the blood would not drain away. He killed the others in order of size, the smallest last. I noticed how quiet it was. I was surprised how natural and ungory the whole process had seemed. Some young men gathered sticks to build a fire. One by one the pigs were laid on bamboo poles over the fire and scraped with wooden instruments to remove the hair. Dennis Hopper was standing near me. He was telling me how he kills pigs in New Mexico with a .22 pistol and covers them with shaving cream and shaves the hair off.

The largest pig was hoisted up into the house of the head priest. The others were butchered by the remaining men on the mat under the house. The little kids were given the pigs' feet to play with. Various cuts of meat went to the different households, depending on their status in the community. A big caldron was put on the fire and pieces of pork were put in it to boil.

The mayor told me that they were also going to kill a carabao for the feast, so I decided to go back to the house to see if Francis wanted to come and see that. When I got home, Francis was down in his room trying to write. The air conditioner was on full blast and the electric typewriter was humming, but he was lying on the couch, stuck and miserable. He came with me, out to the set. The carabao was tied to a nearby tree. Two priests came out from under the house and stood chanting about twenty feet from the carabao. I was fussing around with my camera, trying to get a shot with Francis, the priests and the carabao, all in the frame. Suddenly, I heard a rush from behind me, and four men with bolo knives ran past and began whacking at the carabao. It was a big animal and it was down and dead and being butchered in the course of two or three minutes. The tail was given to the children watching. The entrails were removed. There was the carcass, with a man scooping out the remaining handfuls of blood into a yellow plastic bucket. The animal was quartered and carried to the shade under the house. Little kids stuck their fingers into the windpipe of the head and played around.

In a little while, several very large flat baskets of cooked rice were brought out and placed on the ground. The boys gathered around one and the little girls and old women around the other. Pieces of the cooked pork were given out and the people squatted by the rice, eating with their fingers. I looked at my watch. It was three in the afternoon and I realized I was really hungry. I had a piece of the pork that had been roasted over the fire rather than boiled, and several handfuls of rice. There was no salt on the food, but otherwise it tasted good. There was a joyfulness to the people eating. Maybe it was equivalent to Thanksgiving dinner.

As Francis and I were getting ready to leave, the mayor asked if we would do the priest the honor of accepting the best part of the carabao that is usually reserved for him, the heart. We said yes, so he came out with the heart and several pieces from the loin tied together on a loop of string. It was dripping blood. We thanked him. Through a translator, he said that he would like his picture taken with Francis. I took a photograph of the two priests and Francis standing there together. We put the heart in a cardboard box in the trunk of the car and started home. I gave some meat to our Filipina maid. She tried it and didn't like it, so she put it all in the landlord's freezer.

That evening, Marlon gave a party at the resort where he is staying. He invited all the cast, crew and Ifugaos. Four hundred people came. I was standing out on the grass talking to Albert Hall's wife and looking over her shoulder at the mixture of people in the long line passing the fancy catered buffet tables. Some acts from Manila entertained after dinner. The Ifugaos didn't seem to care much about the disco singers and acrobats, but they crowded in close and were totally attentive while the magician was on. When the entertainers finished, the special effects men set off a fireworks display. The noisy rockets shot out over the lake were the Ifugaos' favorites.

September 10, Pagsanjan

Mary Ellen Mark is here. God! It is good to talk to another woman. She said she brought some new magazines. I could see she thought I would really get excited about that. Actually, our long conversation this morning meant more to me than a thousand fresh news journals.

September 11, Pagsanjan

I am sitting on a bag of tools hidden behind some boxes on the dock at Kurtz Compound. It is the big shot where the PBR approaches and comes through the lines of canoes with natives covered in white mud. It is starting to rain. I can see the makeup men, huddled together, talking over what they should do if the mud starts to wash off the four hundred extras. There is a radio on nearby. The chatter never stops: "More orange smoke, orange smoke. Dead Vietnamese, take your positions. Yellow smoke. Rolling." I am just sitting down a few minutes while Larry has gone back to the truck for more film.

September 14, Pagsanjan

When I got to the set around nine in the evening, the whole crew was waiting. Francis, Marlon and Marty were down on the houseboat talking. The crew had been standing by for about four hours. The propman got a basket of chocolate candy from his truck and passed it around. It had come from the States. The candy kisses I had were sort of that light color chocolate gets when it is old. Sitting there in the damp temple set, that didn't seem to matter to anybody. Finally, at 11:00 P.M., the first assistant called a wrap and everybody went home.

136

Just as I was going to the car, there was a radio message that Francis wanted me to wait for him. I walked down the path near Marlon's houseboat dressing room. The bodyguards and drivers and the wardrobe and makeup people were waiting for Francis and Marlon and Marty. We stood around and talked for about an hour and then the wardrobe and makeup men went home. It was starting to rain again, so I decided to go down to the boat and interrupt them and see if I couldn't get them to finish up. I was really sleepy and my clothes were wet and soggy. When I got to the houseboat, I thought for a moment maybe they were asleep or gone. The light was low and I couldn't see anyone. They were down in the back, sitting by the table. When I went in, I felt like I was slicing into their conversation. The air was like a solid mass of words. I started to wake up immediately. I sat down next to Marlon on the couch, only I miscalculated and sat halfway on a tray of leftover dinner. I never do those kinds of things. Being in Marlon's presence is not neutral. I do things or say things that I wouldn't ordinarily. What a burden it must be for him to hardly have anyone who feels completely natural around him.

September 16, Pagsanjan

Last night Francis climbed up a scaffolding onto a lighting platform and just lay there. It was raining lightly, and when I climbed up, it was wet with standing puddles on top. He was about as miserable as I have ever seen him. It was his ultimate nightmare. He was on this huge set of this huge production with every asset mortgaged against the outcome; hundreds of crew members were waiting. Brando was due on the set and he was delaying because he didn't like the scene, and Francis hadn't been able to write a scene that Marlon thought was really right. The ultimate actor on the ultimate set of the ultimate production with the ultimate cinematographer, and Francis with no scene to play. He kept saying, "Let me out of here, let me just quit and go home. I can't do it. I can't see it. If I can't see it, I can't do anything. This is like an opening night; the curtain goes up and there is no show."

Vittorio came out from the interior of the temple where he was lighting and said, "Look, Francis, I think we can do something. I have made some strange light and smoke and I think you can do something." Finally Francis dragged himself back inside. Marlon came and they began doing an improvisation and shooting that. After the third take, it was midnight and they wrapped.

Francis was starting to feel better. It seemed to me that what was getting him down was that his talent is the ability to discriminate, the ability to see a moment of truthful acting and distinguish it from all the others. Since Brando hadn't started to work, there was nothing for Francis to use to lead him to the next moment and the next. As soon as Brando started to improvise, Francis could begin to direct, that is, see the direction the scene should go. Today he wrote a scene based on the improvisation. He is starting to see it.

September 21, Pagsanjan

I am in the kitchen. Sofia is making a pizza out of play dough. She is painting chunks yellow for cheese, red for tomatoes and green for peppers. The flour has weevils in it. I guess it's been in the canister since Manila. Now and then a groggy weevil gets up out of one of the pieces and walks off across the tray.

Francis, Marlon and Marty are in the living room talking about today's scene. I just brought Marty some coffee. I thought about women's lib. Here I am in the kitchen with the kid, making coffee.

I can hear parts of the conversation coming from the other room. "Don't you see, Kurtz is caught in this conflict of . . ." A truck just passed by, the chickens are crowing next door and the landlord's radio is blaring, Glen Campbell is singing "I'm a Rhinestone Cowboy."

September 22, Pagsanjan

Dennis Jakob just arrived with a suitcase filled with fruit and vegetables from Napa. We opened it up on the living room floor. It looks like a sculpture, blue Samsonite filled with ripe oranges, green apples, plum tomatoes, a plastic bag full of roses, containers of figs and grapes, fresh basil and chives. I am thinking about leaving it right where it is.

September 29, Pagsanjan

I am sitting on a rock on the set. It feels like a rock, it looks like a temple fragment, but I know it was made by the art department. The crew has been waiting since 8:00 A.M. to shoot. It is almost three in the afternoon now. Francis and Marlon have been down in his houseboat, working out his death scene today, and most of yesterday. The assistant director is saying that if they don't start shooting in the next thirty minutes, it will be too late to get a shot today: "Eighty thousand dollars down the drain."

September 30

Yesterday I was standing on the dock at the set, watching the second unit shoot. They were placing Vietnamese extras on the steps of Monkey Island and pouring blood on them. There were dummies floating in heaps in the water lilies. Special effects fires were burning, and about 150 Ifugaos were placed along the far shore and among the sandbags along the wall behind me. The shot was a point of view for the PBR as it approaches Kurtz Compound. The exhaust from the engines was floating in a misty trail behind the boat. It was late afternoon and the light and smoke looked theatrical. I began thinking that it was like being in a theater that was a full 360 degrees around me. Dennis, the boat gaffer, was sitting on a box a few feet from me, keeping his eye on the camera barge. He said, "You know, Ellie, I discovered this great salad dressing. You get a container of sour cream from Manila and the same amount of mayonnaise and mix it together with about half a cup of Parmesan cheese and some garlic salt; it's great! Just like you'd get at Rubin's Steak House in L.A. or someplace like that."

October 8

This is the last day that Marlon works. The shot is outside by the CONEX container. This morning it was warm and sort of tropical and balmy, not miserably hot. Francis and Marlon were talking out the scene. I got a couple of shots of them at a distance, sitting outside an Ifugao house, deep in discussion. It started to rain and everybody began to cover equipment. Now it is pouring. Francis and Marlon and Marty are crouched under an Ifugao house. I am sitting under a lighting reflector, quite comfortably. Some of my equipment got wet before I could get it covered. The crew is all huddled in little bunches under things. Bill and Jimmy Keane are under here with me. We've been talking about the Metropolitan Museum of Art. Jimmy was an elevator operator at the hotel where we stay in New York. He is talking about all the famous people he met who came to the hotel while he worked there. He said his favorite was Frank Capra, the director. "A little fellow, well over four feet."

I can see some big hunks of clear sky across the river. I

can imagine Francis's tension, sitting out the rain when this is the last day Marlon works and there is a scene left to get.

I am listening to the sound of the rain hitting the reflector and watching all the little dramas of the other groups of people huddled together. The Italians started a dice game under the umbrella with the arc light. The prop- and wardrobe men are pitching little rocks, trying to hit a metal container. They are making bets and running out into the rain to get fresh supplies of rocks. Mario is getting a back rub from one of the Filipino electricians. Jimmy is talking about Monte Cristo cigars. The bottom of my shelter is starting to run with mud.

October 9, Pagsanjan

Today Bill and I have been shooting around the house. Sofia is coloring at the table in the living room. She is impatient about my shooting. She keeps asking when I'm going to stop and play with her. She made a pin-the-nose-on-the-clown game and stuck it on the refrigerator. We stopped for a few minutes and took a turn with the blindfold, playing the game. I shot some footage of Ester washing our clothes at the faucet in the backyard and hanging *Apocalypse Now* T-shirts on the clothesline.

October 11

When Marlon finished his last shot on Friday, Francis embraced him and then jumped into the helicopter, headed for the Manila Airport and a 6:00 P.M. flight to Hong Kong. He went with Dean. People kept asking me why I didn't go. I didn't go because Francis wanted, and needed, a couple of days of total escape from everything here, including me. I have been twice, and I didn't especially want to go. This is such a closed society. I could see several people speculating as to why I really didn't go.

I spent the weekend with Sofia. She is terrific company. We made things and went walking. I had never walked through Pagsanjan. I am always rushing off in a jeep, or sitting inside the air-conditioned car. Walking, I could see all the little details of life here. Feeding the chickens, pounding the clothes at the washing faucet, stacking up coconut husks, making a charcoal fire, buying a little sack of rice and some dried fish at a stand, drawing on the road with a rock, waving the baby's hand at passersby.

We stopped at a bakery and bought a *pan dulce*, a big one for about 6 cents, and pulled off chunks as we went along. It was hot. I brought the umbrella. We passed many people with bright-colored umbrellas, backlit in the afternoon sun. The incredible heat seems to have passed. It rains almost every day now. We walked to the Falls Lodge and went swimming in the mineral pools. All along the way, people would call out "Sofia" or "Mees Coppola." I felt that I couldn't just walk along lost in my own thoughts, because I might accidentally ignore someone who was trying to be cordial.

October 15

Thirty-eight takes, and Francis said it was never the way he wanted it. The people who were playing the severed heads sat in their boxes, buried in the ground, from eight in the morning till six at night. All day they were there in the hot sun, with smoke blowing on them. Between takes they were covered with umbrellas. They got out for lunch, but the rest of the time they were there in place.

During one take, Dennis Hopper backed up and stepped right at a girl's cheek and collapsed part of the container she was in, nearly stepping on her face. The mud on both sides of the dolly track was deep and people kept slipping. Dennis and Fred Forrest both fell during takes. The sound man had someone hold on to his belt in the back and stabilize him as he followed the actors, so that he wouldn't fall with the boom.

It was one of those days where the dry ice mist, or the orange smoke, or the performance, or the light, or something just never came together for a take that Francis was satisfied with.

At one point I was sitting there looking around. The severed heads were drinking Cokes. The Ifugao children were putting chunks of dry ice in film cans and making the lids pop off. Some Ifugao girls were picking lice out of each other's hair. One girl had a wrapped skirt, bare breasts and pink plastic hair rollers. A man sitting down in his loincloth held up the fringed ends neatly so they wouldn't get in the mud. The man with the boa constrictor was giving it a drink of water. Alex was talking about the fake blood . . . "It's thirty-five dollars a gallon and they're really using a lot today." Special effects ran out of orange smoke and had to use red. My favorite old Ifugao priest wasn't in costume today; he had on a loincloth and beige print, nylon jersey sport shirt. He came up close to the steps to take a look at the fake severed heads. They say his tribe were headhunters as recently as five years ago. Angelo had a tuna sandwich he was passing around, and people were saying, "You know how long it's been since I had a tuna sandwich?"

October 17, Pagsanjan

I shot an interview with Dennis Hopper. One of the things he said that interested me the most was that he thought filmmaking was in the same phase of development that art was during the cathedral-building period. When they built those great cathedrals in Europe, they employed stonemasons, engineers, fresco painters, etc., and created the work through the combined talents of many. By the nineteenth century, art evolved to the point where the major work of the day was being done by individual artists working alone at an easel. Dennis was making the point that now filmmaking involves the talents of many departments and perhaps eventually major films will be made by one person with a video port-a-pack.

October 20, Pagsanjan

Last night Francis got in a rage because people wandered into the screening room while the rushes were being screened. There is such a magnetic draw to watch. When people make some little inane comment later, it really sets Francis's equilibrium off. It sets his self-destructive stuff in action, his self-doubt.

October 25, Pagsanjan

I am sitting on the temple steps. It is five thirty in the evening, the shooting is finished for the day. The light is going earlier now as if winter were coming, but today was as hot as it's ever been. I love this time of day. The light is soft and starting to obscure the edges of things. Francis and Vittorio are walking the shot for tomorrow. It involves a long and complicated dolly and Alfredo and Luciano are standing by Vittorio getting their instructions.

I can hear the Ifugaos chopping wood for their evening fires.

Last night we went to Vittorio's house for dinner. It was hot. We were sitting outside in the front yard, hoping for some slight current of air. There was only the pungent

146

smell of burning mosquito coils. We could hear sounds of voices in the distance. In a little while a religious procession passed by on the road. It was dark and each person was carrying a lighted candle. I could see faces in the flickering light. There were a lot of really young children. They were singing softly. After about fifty people passed, a little float on wheels came by. It was pushed by four men. On it was a five-foot Virgin all lit up with lights. There were fluorescent tubes in the base. Next a big group passed that included nuns and a boy carrying a loudspeaker. About fifty feet behind was a priest saying a Rosary into the microphone. Then a float with the Virgin of Guadalupe and more elaborate sprays of lighted plastic flowers. Behind that came some men pushing a noisy generator on a little wooden cart.

We had dinner with Giovanni, Sofia, Vittorio and Luciano and his wife. It was sad with Gio and Roman gone, and Tonia, Francesca and Fabrizio are in Rome. The dinner table seemed quiet and missing a liveliness we had together before. After dinner we watched stills that Vittorio had taken during the shooting. It was amazing to see shots isolated; Francis got excited. He kept saying, "God! I'd go to see that movie, wouldn't you?" Being on the set every day we get immune to the incredible imagery. Also, Vittorio's slides are extraordinary. There were a couple that I have been seeing in my mind's eye all day today. One with a double exposure: Martin's head against a black background, with Marlon and the Ifugao children superimposed clearly over his brain.

October 26, Pagsanjan

Yesterday Sofia lost her first tooth. The last few days, while she was wiggling it, I thought more than once about my last child leaving babyhood. She wanted me to type a letter to the tooth fairy. She dictated it while I typed:

I am Sofia. I lost my tooth when I was swimming at Lake Caliraya, so now I cannot give you the tooth. So I am giving you a letter for you will know that I lost my tooth. The next time I will try to get the tooth and put it under my pillow. I hope you can give me a surprise even though I don't have the tooth right under my pillow. I am a girl.

She went in to take a nap. She kept calling me, asking me questions: "Does the tooth fairy have blond hair?" "Does she have a crown?" "Why do fairies have crowns?" "Maybe because a kid might think it's his parents leaving the present."

Finally she went to sleep and I went out to the Chinese grocery store to see what I could find in the way of a surprise. I bought a little plastic bag with a balloon, gum and candy in it, a box of crayons, some Johnson's baby cologne, new thongs and a piece of flowered wrapping paper. It was hard to find those things among the canned goods, coils of rope, candles, kerosene, Cokes, underwear, socks, T-shirts, cookies, hardware, etc. I went home and wrapped the package and put it under her pillow. Then I went out to the set to see how Francis was doing. When I came home, Sofia was really excited about the tooth fairy's visit. She showed me each thing, looking it over carefully. She said, "You know, Mom, I think she was a Filipina fairy with short black hair."

October 27, Pagsanjan

There was a production meeting last night to go over the schedule. If there are no delays due to the rain, the last day of shooting will be December 24.

I've just come back from the set. I wanted to get some shots of Alfredo completing the bridge he started yesterday for the long dolly shot tracking past the whole front of Kurtz Compound. For me, he really is a sculptor of wood and metal. Francis came out in the middle of the track and shook his hand. Alfredo is not pompous, but there is an air of confidence and satisfaction that he can create the means for the director to get a complicated shot he wants.

It has been raining hard this morning. Francis has had to set up a shot inside the temple in order not to lose the morning. Alfredo and his men have on raincoats and some of the Filipinos are wearing plastic bags around their shoulders. Larry was holding the umbrella so that my camera wouldn't get wet. It started to pour and during the last few shots I got soaked. The umbrella only covered the camera and my head; everything else got wet. Finally we gave up and went back to the car to take the equipment home and dry it out. It began raining harder and harder. Areas of the set were completely obscured. As we drove away I kept looking back at how beautiful it was. Larry and I were talking about how you can only see rain on film when it is superheavy like this. We had gone about a quarter of a mile and I realized that we should go back and try to get some shots from the temple. To really show the rain. I had the driver turn around. By the time we got back and set up in a doorway of the temple, the heavy rain had stopped. I was mad at myself for not being able to switch my mind set from the preconception of going home to staying and shooting the rain. The delay in recognizing the opportunity at the moment had cost me the shot. That is one of the most frustrating aspects of documentary filmmaking for me—the way my mind gets a fix on what I plan to shoot and the time it takes me to let go of that preconception in favor of something that might be far more interesting.

October 28

Francis got the last shot yesterday at 5:00 P.M. and we hopped into the helicopter waiting on the set and flew to Manila. It was the first time I'd been up since we flew back from Iba during the typhoon. It seemed new again, seeing everything from the air. The fish traps looked like great designs etched on blue silver. There were patterns of boncas on the shore, and ships at anchor in Manila Bay. Roxas Boulevard, with its hotels and traffic, looked exotic and exciting after Pagsanjan. The helicopter landed in the street right at the front door of the Manila Hotel. I jumped out and opened the suitcase in the luggage compartment and took out Francis's shoes so he could change from his muddy boots before we went in. There were several porters and doormen in new starched white uniforms. The manager of the hotel was waiting for us. We were shown to our rooms. I realized I still had on my muddy boots. I tried not to step on the carpet.

The hotel was built in 1910 and is just reopening, newly remodeled. It is a tasteful blend of old and new. Our room had nice wicker chairs, a Victorian marble-topped coffee table and handwoven fabrics framed on the walls. Actually, it was the bathtub that we both flashed on most. I hadn't had a bath for about three months. Francis was the dirtiest, so he got the first one. I sat in front of the air conditioner and let myself get really cold. When Francis was out of the tub I took a long, hot bath. I loved lying there with the water filled to the top, as hot as I could stand it. I could hear the TV in the other room. Francis was watching *Batman*. We went to dinner at our favorite Japanese restaurant. The sashimi was perfect. We had four orders.

This morning I woke up at six and placed a call to the boys. I was really excited about talking to them. The call never came through, and at seven thirty we had to leave. The helicopter picked us up. At eight we landed at Kurtz Compound and walked through the mud to the first camera position.

November 2

Sunday was Halloween. I took Sofia to Manila so she could go trick-or-treating with Claire at the houses of American families in Dasmariñas. The ride in was nice. Sofia fell asleep on my lap. It was late afternoon, the light was beautiful, I just looked out the window at all the events along the road. Each town was preparing for All Saints' Day, November 1. It is one of the biggest holidays of the year here. At each cemetery, people were painting and washing the grave markers, and food stalls were setting up along the outside walls. The larger towns had rickety Ferris wheels and carnival games. Twice we passed funeral processions. One I could see pretty well. There was a shiny, glass-paneled station wagon with the casket and flowers. It was followed by people walking. The immediate family, dressed in black, walked first, then came friends and finally a little brass band wearing patched khaki uniforms. The station wagon was having a hard time going slow enough for the people walking. Now and then it would stall and have to start up again, belching a cloud of black exhaust at the mourners.

The road to Manila passes through five or six regional districts. Each one had roadside stands selling the local specialty. We passed stands selling carabao cheese wrapped in neat little banana leaf packages, an area where they sell scrap rubber and used tires, then stalls and stalls of Buko pie, made from coconuts. There was a place with stores selling decor for jeepneys, all those hood and dashboard decorations, like silver horses, Jesus pictures and girls' names spelled out in red plastic fringe. There was an area of fruit stands, selling baskets of lanzones, a local fruit too sour and full of seeds for my taste, but Sofia likes it a lot.

We passed a bunch of kids flying kites in a green rice field. They looked like a picture from some United Nations greeting card, except for the sign advertising the name of the pesticide used in the field. My friend Arlene told me that most of the pesticides they use here are banned in the United States.

When we got to Manila it was early evening. I dropped Sofia at her friend's house and went to check into a hotel. I walked around and went shopping until it was time to go back for her. When I arrived to pick her up, Claire's father asked me to stay for dinner. He fixed me a vodka and tonic, and we drank and watched the kids in their costumes sorting through the candy in their Halloween bags. Then we sat down to dinner. They said grace and served Shakey's pizza, followed by brownies and ice cream. I was sitting at the head of the table and as I looked around at the McGinitys and their three blond children, my vodka tonic, pizza and brownies, it seemed as exotic as anything I'd seen lately.

The next day, I had Claire come to the hotel and play by the pool with Sofia. Once in a while I would hear part of their conversation. They talked about politics. Claire said, "My president isn't President Marcos, mine is President Forb." They talked about what foods they liked and what ones they didn't like. Finally, Sofia said, "Well, you know, cockroaches like to eat anything."

In the evening Sofia and I took a taxi to the office and got on the crew bus returning to Pagsanjan. As the bus drove out of Manila, we passed a large city cemetery. There was a big crowd and the traffic slowed down to a crawl. The cemetery was lit up with bare light bulbs and thousands of candles. Being up high in the bus, I could see the details of the graveyard, the people, the food stands and the little carnivals.

Sofia had fallen asleep on the seat beside me. I was looking out the window into the night. The imagery we passed was so strong I began thinking about my friend Ed telling me that the things we see around us are not just arbitrary. They can be interpreted, sort of the way you interpret a dream. You can get pertinent information about what is going on in your life by looking at the events occurring around you. I began thinking about what the cemeteries and celebrations symbolized in my life, and why I was seeing them just now.

Actually, the reason I went to Manila was because Francis went away for a few days and I didn't want to stay alone in Pagsanjan. I wanted to do something and be diverted from thinking about him. Francis has been in such anguish lately, so angry: angry at the movie, angry with me, angry with his family, angry with everybody that works for him, angry at his life. So he went away to be completely alone and try to figure out what is bothering him so much.

Lately, it seems like he has been struggling with his expectations of *how he thinks* his life and the people in it are supposed to be, versus how things actually are. Some beliefs and attitudes and expectations he has had since childhood seem to be dying. There is a lot of grief and anger and fear associated with death.

The people I was seeing out the window, in the cemeteries, were paying respects to the dead, to the past, and then celebrating the present. It seemed as though it symbolized something about death, it was a little distance from me, perhaps pertaining to Francis, but it was not sad, it was somehow cause for celebration.

November 3, Pagsanjan

Francis came home early this morning. He hugged and kissed me and said everything was all right. He had figured it out. He said that ever since he was a little kid he had wanted to be talented and successful, and win the approval of his family and friends and women. He wanted, most of all, to be really talented, and he had always doubted he was, so the approval he got made him sort of miserable because it seemed like a lie. Well, he said, what he realized was that he *is* talented, but not in the ways he expected, not in the ways he thought he was, not like in his childhood fantasies. Not in traditional ways. He said he thought his actual talents lay in areas of conceptualizing, of seeing something, seeing how something could be done, adapting ideas in new ways, innovating, instead of building something from scratch. He said he thought the areas of his abilities didn't fit neatly into the traditional concept of the movie industry, and perhaps that is why he intuitively left the Los Angeles movie world. Maybe he could never seem to get his plans for a film studio off the ground because being head of a studio was mostly a preconception of what you do if you are a success in the movie business. He said

154

maybe the reason this film has been so hard for him, and why he has been so miserable, is because the traditional ways he *thought* he should be working weren't panning out and he was really angry and scared. When in truth, his best work on the film was conceptual and innovative and couldn't have been done in a traditional way. He said that usually a script is complete and decisive before shooting starts, but now, he could see that the improvisations and fumbling he has done have produced some of the best scenes so far. Marlon was supposed to be lean and hard in order to play a Green Beret officer, but when he arrived hopelessly overweight, he had to give up his preconceptions about the character and come up with a solution which pushed the film much more in the direction of a myth and turned out to be better than his original concept. He said he began to realize that a good director might not be the one who was completely prepared and definitive, but one who could take the situations that happen and utilize them to his advantage rather than close down the production until events matched his original plans. He said he realized that he always had new ideas and solutions. That when the typhoon hit, he didn't stop shooting immediately; he changed the scene to include a storm. He said he was always angry with himself about how slow the shooting was going. A lot of it was because the Italian crew and Vittorio worked in different ways than American crews. He said he felt it was his fault for not keeping a proper pace. Now he realized that Vittorio and the style of shooting were key concepts of the film. By his nontraditional choice of a cinematographer he was making a better film. He said he thought he was actually making the film well, using his real talents, just not doing it the way he *thought* a good director should be doing it. He was excited about the possibility of exploring his talent where he feels it really lies, seeing his life the way it is and letting go of his preconceptions.

November 4, Pagsanjan

We found out Sofia has lice. I gave her a shampoo with this real strong-smelling stuff, and last night Francis sat on the couch with her head in his lap, looking through her hair with a flashlight for the tiny eggs.

November 5, Pagsanjan

Francis came home at lunchtime. He was talking about ideas he had for films that could be six minutes, forty-seven minutes or two and a half hours long. That he could make in three days, or three weeks or one week with a real fast crew. Maybe he'd use a news team. He was really excited about making films that he called "spatial" instead of linear story films.

Finally someone came to the door to say that he was needed on the set. As he was leaving he said, "Ellie, remember that fat guy who wore those kind of funny-looking corduroy suits and walked around North Beach like a bohemian? I think he died."

November 6, Pagsanjan

Francis: "I don't make the person play the part, I make the part play the person. People think that you only do that with nonactors. It works great with actors."

November 7, Pagsanjan

It is Sunday. Vittorio and Dean came for breakfast. Francis made omelets with Swiss cheese and fresh basil. The Swiss cheese cost nearly $15 for one good-sized chunk from the imported food section of the supermarket in Manila. The basil was from a pot that we've finally gotten to grow. After breakfast we took Giovanni and Sofia with us and went to the Tropical Hotel to meet the helicopter, go up and look for a river location that the company could use when it comes back after Christmas as a smaller unit. The helicopter was late. Francis, Dean and Vittorio sat on the curb talking. Francis was saying, "We are the three guys making this picture." They were sitting in front of a wall of cases of empty Coke bottles on the sidewalk. I took some stills.

Giovanni was getting excited about going up in the helicopter and running around acting crazy. Sofia found some broken glass in the street and cut her finger. Finally, the helicopter landed and we went up. I had a rush of excitement as we rose, and the view of the world literally changed. I love the patterns of the rice paddies from the air. We flew over a river; looking down you could see that the water was too shallow for the PBR. In the distance we saw a puff of white cloud near a mountain. The pilot said it was a volcano. We decided to fly over and have a look. It was live and we could smell the sulfur as we flew by. We could see the molten rock bubbling and steaming in the crater. We flew to Lucena and followed some of the rivers that flow into the sea in that area. We were banking and turning and dipping down to look at some inlet or other and I was starting to feel sick. I could see that Giovanni was looking pale, too, so Francis asked the pilot to land somewhere so we could get out for a few minutes. The helicopter set down on a little beach and we just rolled out and lay on the sand for a while. The beach was totally deserted when we arrived, but people started coming from all directions and gathering around the helicopter and looking at us. The kids were playing in the sand. Francis started to tell me this whole story of his childhood. After a while I looked up and noticed that Dean had drawn a picture of a helicopter in the sand and a soldier firing a gun, with dotted lines for the bullets that ended up right at Francis. I don't know how long we had been lying there talking. We realized how good we all felt. It was because the air was a perfect temperature. Not too hot, maybe about 75 degrees. Just perfect. A breeze was coming off the water, and it wasn't muggy.

The people waved to us as we lifted off. We were home in about fifteen minutes. I've got to go up with the camera and get some shots before I leave. The patterns and shapes from the air are such an art show for me.

November 9, Pagsanjan

I went to look for Francis on the set. The assistant director said he was in Palm Springs. I found out that is what Francis's little dressing room hut is now called. I went in. It was hotter than Palm Springs by a long shot. Francis was listening to his tape recorder while he was waiting for the next shot setup. Beethoven was turned up pretty loud. He was talking about music being the most perfect time-space sculpture . . . and maybe movies. It was nice sitting in there, in the dark. I was listening and looking at the stars of light coming through the weave of the mat walls.

November 9

Last Saturday, Dennis Hopper finished. Francis decided to get drunk with him to celebrate. They started on wine and coconut liquor. Francis threw the first empty wine bottle up in the air behind him. It flew across the room and bounced along the terrazzo floor. People began dropping in. Around thirty people were helping themselves to whatever drinks they could find. Pretty soon there was no more cold beer or much else to drink. I noticed I was starting to feel sort of panicked. Nobody was taking care of what was going on in the kitchen. I was talking to Caterine on the couch. She gave me some of her slides and an autographed copy of her book. She was showing me her journal, tidbits of everything, notes, a drawing by Sofia, some Polaroid shots of her and Dennis wearing hats and no clothes. I didn't get up to play hostess. Pete Cooper started making Bloody Marys with some canned V-8 juice we brought from San Francisco.

Several production people came in and said that Dennis had to leave immediately to get to Manila before curfew because he had a 6:00 A.M. flight to Hamburg. He was already three days late to his next assignment. Dennis was pretty drunk and in no mood to leave. Francis said, "Dennis, pick anyplace in the world, you'll be the star of a movie I'll make. The deal is, I promise I won't think about what the movie is going to be before we start. We'll just make it, we'll make it real fast, in three weeks, and it will be terrific. Pick a place." Dennis was saying, "Okay, okay, yeah." Francis and I waited to hear what exotic place it was going to be. Finally, Dennis said, "San Francisco." He said his wife and child were there and her parents. Francis said, "Okay, that's the story, that's where the story is. We'll do it." The production guy whose responsibility it was to get Dennis to Manila was getting pale. I asked Francis to help get Dennis going. Finally, after another half hour of noise and hugging and kissing and carrying on, Dennis and Caterine got into the car and on their way.

The people who had gathered at our house began drifting off to a party at Lake Caliraya for some young women who were visiting exchange students from the United States. I saw them walking around the set during the day. They looked like a nice group of senior Girl Scouts from the Midwest. The crew seemed very anxious to meet them. Francis went along, too. I went into the kitchen and made myself some dinner and was in bed reading by eleven thirty. I fell asleep. I guess Francis came to bed around two or three.

The next morning I was buying some bananas from the stand across the street. The ladies were saying, "That was quite a party you had at your house last night." I said that yes, I guess it was a bit rowdy. But that wasn't what they

were talking about; they were totally knocked out because
Francis had started barbecuing at 1:00 A.M., making dinner
for himself. Barbecuing in the middle of the night, after
curfew, was apparently really big news. The landlord men-
tioned it, too.

November 10, Pagsanjan

This evening I was waiting at the production office for the
mail to come in. I felt silly, as though I had no business
wasting my time doing that. I hadn't waited for mail since
Girl Scout camp. Finally, the driver arrived from Manila
and one of the office girls sorted through the package of
letters for me before she put it into the crew mailboxes. I
got a letter from my mother. Francis and I got an invitation
from the Marchese and Marchesa Gino Cacciapouti Di
Giugliano to the wedding of their daughter Miss Marisa
Schiaparelli Berenson to Mr. James H. Randall. I have
never met them. I think Francis has met Marisa. Francis
got two letters from the law offices of Schiff, Hirsch and
Schreiber, and a handwritten book, by somebody he never
heard of. The book was one of those black sketchbooks
with blank pages. In it was a hand-printed story about two
dogs that lived in San Francisco named Francis and Ford.

I was hoping for a letter from Gio and Roman.

November 11, Pagsanjan

Last night was one of those evenings of night shooting that really knocked me out. Just going down the last stretch of road with the temple all lit up below was really exciting. I felt like I was going to some incredible theater performance. Like going to see *Aida* at the Baths of Caracalla when I was eighteen and away in a foreign land for the first time. I didn't know what to expect, anything was possible, live horses or elephants or anything could come thundering across the stage. It felt like that. It was raining lightly. I had on my boots and I walked out through the mud to where Francis and Dean were talking in front of the temple. Francis had just decided that Willard should come up out of a primeval swamp, and about twenty-five laborers had already begun digging out an area to be filled with water. It had to be ready in about three hours, completely finished with the shrubs and plants and grass for the first shot. Dean was directing his crew to place the wooden sculptures for the Killing of the Carabao Festival that was going to be part of the background for the shot. In between, Francis and Dean were talking about a film they would make where Dean would do a set that was a perfect replica of one square block of New York City, complete with traffic and polluted air and everything, only he would make it in Arizona somewhere. Then Francis would make a film. But the money for the film would only go to pay for the block of New York to remain as a sculpture in Arizona. Sort of the reverse of Christo.

Dean had to go do something and Francis started talking about one of the next films he is going to make, telling me how he had seen a series of scenes in his mind's eye. It was interesting to hear about it. Big visual chunks of the movie had come to him. He said it was like watching the film as if it already existed. I started to wonder if it does already exist

and all Francis is doing is putting it together. We have
wondered about this film. On the first of September there
was no ending for this film and now there is. Where did it
come from? Francis didn't write it, it sort of happened, day
by day, and it is completely different and better than any
of the endings he wrote on for over a year.

We were talking about all kinds of things. We were standing there in the mud in the middle of the set. Francis's
bodyguard was standing right behind him, holding an umbrella over us. He turned his head to the side so that he
wasn't staring at us, but he heard everything.

The shot for the evening had a long dolly setup that
traveled over a hundred feet under four Ifugao houses. We
were under there, sitting by the track, with our feet in
chicken dung or something that really smelled. Alfredo was
saying something in Italian, laughing about look how Mr.
Coppola has us down under here working in this shit. Francis said, "Well, that's life." And Alfredo said, "No, that's
not life, that's the movie business. In life I have a nice place
that smells good."

Everybody was working hard. There was a kind of excitement, like at Do Long Bridge the first night. I don't know
what it was. Maybe it was Vittorio's lighting and the Ifugaos
dancing, the rain and the mud and chicken shit, and the
fires, skulls, candles, the temple and wooden totems, banners, ducks, sandbags, coconut trees, rubber machine
guns, radio chatter and hot chocolate.

For Francis it was a good night's work. For me it was
theater, terrific theater..

November 13, Pagsanjan

Last night we went down to the set for a party Eva had
arranged for the Ifugaos. She asked them what they would
like; they said American food and ice cream. They have no
refrigeration where they live, up on the rice terraces.

Most of the Ifugaos had on Western clothes. It was
strange to see them in drip-dry outfits instead of loincloths.
I had my camera and was trying to get a shot of them
passing the buffet table with its silver chafing dishes and
flower arrangements, selecting their dinners. One old war-
rior put a big scoop of ice cream on top of the cucumbers
on his paper plate.

Francis presented the tribe with an 8-mm camera, film
and projector. I don't know what the translator told them
about the gift, but they laughed a lot. After dinner there
were songs and dances. Sofia liked the dancing and the
sound of the rhythm instruments. She didn't want to leave,
but Francis wanted to get back to the house because he had
promised to show Dean and Alex a print of *Easy Rider*. We
went home. They were already waiting. We watched the
film on a section of white wall for a screen. A lizard must
have been attracted to the light. It crawled over the image
for quite a while. In the middle of the second reel the
electricity went off. We lit some candles and sat around
waiting. Francis started singing hit tunes from musicals and
finally ended up doing imitations of hits of the fifties. He
did a pretty good Nat King Cole singing "Too Young."
Finally, it was apparent that the electricity was off for the
night. I walked out to the car with Dean and Alex. The
town was completely dark. There was a cool breeze blowing. It wasn't humid, the air was fresh and warm at the
same time. When I went in, Francis was already asleep. I
opened all the windows in the bedroom. It was the first
night we slept without the air conditioner on. This morning

we didn't wake up in a sweat. The cool air is still here. Maybe the seasons are changing at last. The peanut crop and the beans and eggplant, I see from the window, have come and gone in the backyard garden. But a new crop is already in, everything is still lush and green, although the sun sets earlier and the light is different. I do feel a change all around me.

November 14, Pagsanjan

Today Francis was talking about how he doesn't ever match down in a scene. If he has a master shot with something he changes in the close-up, he never tries to make the good film conform to the less good. He stops and makes it all conform to the piece that evolved to be better, or he tries to get around it in the editing. "All that matters is what's on the screen. Nobody cares about what you cut away and whether it matched or not."

November 17, Pagsanjan

Today it is still raining. I was talking to Francis about it this morning. He was saying that there has been some really difficult obstacle during each phase of making this film. In Baler it was the helicopters, at Iba it was the typhoon, at the French plantation it was the actors, at Kurtz Compound, in the beginning it was Marlon, then it was Dennis Hopper and not having a scripted ending. Now it is physical difficulties. There has never been a day when you just went to work, worked real hard, got what was intended and that was that. Tonight there are going to be one thousand extras for the big shot in front of the temple. It is raining hard. There will be more mud than ever.

November 21, Pagsanjan

Last night the helicopter was supposed to pick Sofia and me up at 5:00 P.M. in Manila. It arrived at 5:30 with a relief pilot I didn't know very well. We were supposed to lift off no later than 5:05 P.M. in order to get to Pagsanjan in daylight. We lifted off anyway. When we got over Laguna Province, it was too dark to find Pagsanjan. When the pilot realized he couldn't find the landing pad, he made an emergency approach and came down in a rice paddy. We stepped out into knee-high mud and waded to the road. We flagged down a jeepney and hired it to drive us home.

Today they are digging the helicopter out. The skids sank several feet into the mud. The pilot said he was afraid to say that it was too late to take off. He was afraid not to bring Mrs. Coppola home as per his instructions.

November 23, Pagsanjan

Last night I was sitting up on a camera platform about
fifteen feet in the air. It was like the perfect front-row balcony seat. I could see the whole theater event going on
right around me. The shot was of Ifugao warriors dancing
around the carabao. When Francis saw the first rehearsal
he got a flash. The Ifugao ritual dance with spears was a
perfect parallel for what was going on inside the temple
with Willard. It was as if the dancers outside the temple
were telling what Willard was doing inside. Ifugao warriors
kill the carabao and Willard kills Kurtz.

Luciano caught a huge eight-inch butterfly that flew into
one of the arc lights. Vittorio was shooting with five cameras at once; he kept checking each one. The temple was
lit up. There were amber gels on the lights, so everything
had a warm, yellow-orange glow. The set really looked extraordinary with giant silk banners, carved wooden totems,
black papier-mâché life-sized carabaos, bright-colored
wood and paper flowers, all backlit.

Dean was fixing little details. One Ifugao had a tear in his
shirt. Dean wanted it changed. He adjusted a basket that
had been moved slightly by an electrician. Details that no
one else could see. There was a certain excitement because
it was the last night the Ifugaos worked; if any shot wasn't
gotten, that was it. The Ifugaos were singing and chanting
between takes. The Ifugao children were falling asleep and
had to be awakened for each shot.

December 28, San Francisco

Since I left Pagsanjan three weeks ago, it's all sort of a blur. Sofia and I came home via Tokyo. I wanted to drink tea in a temple garden and poke around in little hardware stores and stationery shops where schoolchildren buy notebooks. I wanted to look at patterned fabric like the ones you see in old woodcuts. My guide was a lovely young woman who took me to Madison Avenue–type jewelry stores, counters of pearls and watches. She had such a mind set about showing me the best, she couldn't hear what I wanted to do, although she understood English perfectly. I have impressions of taking the train to Kyoto, of eating pickled eel and rice in the diner and looking out the window, seeing a maze of smokestacks and factories with Mount Fuji towering in the background. Kyoto felt wonderful in some way I can't explain. As if I had been there before, or there was something there for me although I couldn't quite define it. London, Paris, Rome, Madrid never felt like that. We went to some temples. It was like visiting a dream. I had seen those places in dark projection room slide shows of long-ago art history classes. It was all familiar but different. As we approached that famous sand and stone garden, I expected Zen serenity. There was a loud PA system making announcements. We visited wonderful wooden temples. We stopped outside at a little shop and had tea and round cookies made on old iron rollers. The man who served us ate Ritz crackers out of a box behind the counter.

Sofia and I arrived in San Francisco very tired and excited to see the boys. It was wonderful; we played around for three days. The kids didn't argue. We went bowling and walked around San Francisco. We went to restaurants. We went to an arcade and played all the new computer games. We looked at the Christmas decorations in the windows and went to the park. We talked and hugged. Then the kids went back to school and I began to unpack and look around the house. Every drawer, every cupboard was a mess. Below the surface of quick cleaning for our return was total chaos. Plumbing needed fixing, there were mice, plants had died. The pool filter didn't work. The telephone was ringing. The front door and the back door were buzzing. Robin had stayed to close up the house in Pagsanjan and I had no help. I fell into a depression. Friends called and I didn't want to see them. I didn't want to talk to anyone or go out. I was mad that I was back with this mountain of household responsibilities. I kept hearing from the office how incredible the shooting was. How exciting the sequence at Village I turned out to be and then Hau Phat topped that. And I was the wife sent home to get the house in order for a family Christmas. I was mad and confused, irritated, stumbling over this big house in my life once again. The freeways and car pools and supermarkets seemed idiotic. People asked me about how it was in the Philippines and wasn't I glad to be back. I felt like I was in a familiar place but didn't speak the language. And then Francis came home and was really high and said that every day had been more spectacular than the previous and that he was happier than he had ever been in his life. I started to cry. A little part of me is still weeping. Being angry that what makes me high is not in my life right now. Not even being sure what it is that would make me high. Knowing that what is in front of me has to be tended to, not resisted or escaped from.

PART TWO

1977

January 5, San Francisco

Last night Francis looked at a rough assembly of footage
downstairs in the screening room, about five hours of film.
Only Dennis and Dean were with him. They must have
had the volume up full, because I could hear the sound
track in the bedroom, two floors above. I fell asleep about
midnight, and when Francis came to bed at 2:00 A.M. or
maybe 3:00 A.M., he was so excited it was like an electrical
charge. I woke right up and couldn't go back to sleep. He
said the film was great, a masterpiece. He said it was all
there. He could see it. He said all he had to do was cut
away the part that wasn't *Apocalypse Now* and there the
film would be. It reminded me of reading somewhere that
Michelangelo said all he did was carve away the stone down
to the skin and there was the statue. Francis was saying,
"Can you imagine, improvising the whole ending and it all
being there, and being great?"

He was never, on any of his films, excited and up like he
is now. He was always a real tortured-sufferer type. I can
see that part of me is thrilled for him, his positiveness and
excitement, and part of me is scared by the change. He has
been changed since those days when he went away by himself over Halloween. He is so different. I notice I am always
looking out of the corner of my eye to see if he is coming
down off his high, back to the old familiar, depressed suf-
ferer I knew for all those years.

January 7, San Francisco

I have been growing increasingly angry and negative recently. It reminds me of how I felt during *Godfather II*.

All the time we have been married I have wanted to do some kind of work. It always took a back seat to whatever Francis was doing, and when we went on location, more or less stopped. Finally, on *Godfather II* it got the most extreme. The things I wanted to do, know about, participate in, that stimulated me, were in San Francisco and Francis was on location. When I was in San Francisco I was frantic because I felt myself losing him. When I went on location I was so angry and resentful because I couldn't find what interested me and yet I couldn't voice my complaints because they sounded ridiculous. There I was, sitting in my air-conditioned suite, traveling the world with a film company, privileged wife of the director, and weeping, feeling like a miserable, indulgent, neurotic, middle-aged woman who couldn't get her act together.

There is part of me that *wants* to work. There I was those nine months in the Philippines, working every day on the documentary. It was stimulating and full of insights for me. I didn't realize it, but that was the first time in our married life that my work part and my marriage part were integrated. Since that stopped, when I came home in December, I have been slowly sliding into a morass of negativity and anger. Now, just understanding it, has lightened me up about a thousand pounds.

January 9, San Francisco

Today we went into the screening room at about 10:30 A.M. and came out at 2:00 P.M. for lunch and went back until 6:00 P.M. this evening. The whole day was spent in the warm darkness watching all the hours of the Hau Phat footage with Barry and the kids. It is going to be cut into a six-minute sequence. I wondered what it does to the kids to sit there watching every take of all eight cameras, the Playboy bunnies bumping and grinding away for hours. The day seemed suspended in the dark and now it is night. The footage was amazing.

February 12, San Francisco

I haven't wanted to write any notes for a month now. I haven't wanted to look at my anxiety. I am in this big house with the children. Francis has gone back to the Philippines for the final weeks of shooting. All the time he was home, he was high every day. He appeared to be wonderful. He played music, he played with the children, he focused on all sorts of little details like helping Sofia with her chopsticks. He had dozens of ideas about the house, the sound system, the flowers, changing the bedroom around. He had ideas about new projects, ideas about his office, ideas about ashtrays, toiletries, toothpick holders, things he had never

paid any attention to before. He watched a lot of footage
from the film. He thought it was great. Everything seemed
wonderful. Now that he is back in the Philippines he is
sending a constant barrage of telexes ordering things,
things for the production and things to furnish the cottage
at the resort where he is staying in Hidden Valley. The lists
include table linens, cooking utensils, fine wines, frozen
steaks, hi-fi equipment. He says he is designing his life to
live every moment magnificently. He says he is directing
better than he ever has in his life and is extending the
schedule to add new scenes.

For the most part, I agree with Francis's vision, but
something about it doesn't feel right to me. There is a kind
of franticness. Everyone else seems to think what he is
doing is just great. If I say anything to the contrary, it is
taken as negativity, disloyalty or jealousy.

Before Francis left, a beautiful actress came to see him.
She told him he was the greatest man on the planet, a
genius, speaking to the minds of millions of people around
the world.

I think that Francis truly is a visionary, but part of me is
filled with anxiety. I feel as though a certain discrimination
is missing, that fine discrimination that draws the line between what is visionary and what is madness. I am terrified.

I consulted the I Ching today. I got number 36, "Darken-
ing of the Light." It said:

"You are in the intolerable position of being under the
authority of forces that are contrary to your principles and
beliefs. . . . There is nothing you can do to change this
situation. . . . The scope of this dark authority is so wide
and because its influence is so pervasive, you will be forced
to accede to its impetus on all levels of your life except the
most personal, you are alone among your acquaintances in
your condemnation of these dark forces. Other people
either condone them or maintain a laissez-faire attitude.
No one would be receptive to any initiatives to change or
destroy the powers that be, at least at present. You must
resign yourself. You must not rock the boat. You must hide
your real feelings. You must be blind to the evil surround-

ing you. This is a shameful time for you. But while being forced into all these sins of omission, you must never allow yourself to fall into a sin of commission."

February 25, San Francisco

The I Ching said not to rock the boat. I didn't heed that advice. I sent a telex to Francis telling him that because I loved him, I would tell him what no one else was willing to say, that he was setting up his own Vietnam with his supply lines of wine and steaks and air conditioners. Creating the very situation he went there to expose. That with his staff of hundreds of people carrying out his every request, he was turning into Kurtz—going too far.

I called him an asshole. I addressed the telex to him with copies to Dean, Vittorio, Dick and the production manager.

I got back an avalanche of anger. Francis felt completely betrayed. Furious that I sent a telex over a wire service that anyone could read. His own wife saying he'd gone too far, just when he felt he was doing his best work. Why hadn't I written a letter, given him a chance to explain?

March 1, San Francisco

Last night Francis called from Manila. He said that Marty had a heart attack, he was alive but in critical condition. He said that he called me because he didn't know if anyone else would be home on Friday night. He needed me to act calmly, to contact Tom and the lawyer with a list of things to do. He said he needed to know if he should try to continue shooting or if that would invalidate the insurance. He wanted to keep working unless he heard otherwise because the company was in a state of shock and needed to focus on the day's shooting to keep up the morale and not fall into chaos. He said the production manager had started drinking and wanted to close down the production. He needed information right away so that he could make some decisions about what to do in case Marty didn't recover, in case he recovered but couldn't work, in case he could work but not for many months. He said that the situation should be kept a total secret until they knew more about Marty's condition and had decided what to do. He said that he felt pretty shaken himself but that he was okay.

March 4

I am on Japan Air Lines. Sofia is asleep on the seat beside me. She has on a pink sleeveless jumper with a yellow,

178

long-sleeved, turtleneck T-shirt and white tights. It was cold when we left San Francisco. I plan to take off her tights and T-shirt just before we land in Manila so she can step off the plane in a sleeveless dress and sandals.

Yesterday I got a call from Tom, telling me that Francis wanted me to come to the Philippines immediately; he couldn't tell me much more, just that I should go as soon as possible.

I am trying not to worry, trying not to have preconceptions about what I will find, how Francis will be, trying to be clear, to meet the moment as well as I can. During the trip I have tried to distract myself, to read, play with Sofia, concentrate on little visual details around me. It is impossible.

March 14, Hidden Valley

It is strange to be back in the Philippines. I have been so focused on what has been going on between Francis and me, I have only intermittently noticed the incredible beauty of where we are. We are staying in Hidden Valley, commuting by car or helicopter to the sets in Pagsanjan. Hidden Valley is a resort inside a volcano. The soil is so rich that the foliage is giant. There are incredible tropical plants with four-foot leaves, orchids, hibiscus, banana and coconut palms, bamboo with bright red stalks, trees with hanging pods that are ground and made into thick hot chocolate, amazingly colorful spiders and bugs. There are mineral pools, pools with soda water coming out of the hillside, waterfalls, warm pools with hot springs bubbling up from the bottom, cool pools, all with sunlight filtering through thick foliage. We have a very comfortable small house with a screened porch, furnished with stuff from the French plantation set, some things we had in Pagsanjan and some of the hotel furniture. There is a comfortable clutter of plants and wicker, little things from China, baskets and books and four chattery parrots we are keeping for the prop department. There are videotapes, records, 16-mm projection, quadraphonic sound. There is an editing room downstairs, and a room for Ester, who takes such good care of us.

This place is a paradise seemingly, but Francis has been going through such heavy numbers that the beauty is only occasionally in focus for me. I guess he has had a sort of nervous breakdown. Perhaps it has been going on, in a way, most of the past year. The film he is making is a metaphor for a journey into self. He has made that journey and is still making it. It is scary to watch someone you love go into the center of himself and confront his fears, fear of failure, fear of death, fear of going insane. You have to fail a little, die a little, go insane a little to come out the other side. The process is not over for Francis.

March 18, Hidden Valley

Last night Francis was in the bathtub. I was sitting on the floor weeping. We were talking about whether to get separated or divorced. Outside the bathroom door two men started arguing about the four-channel recorder in the bedroom. Yelling about punching each other out if the other guy put his finger on it. "My ass is on the line."

This weekend Francis and I are having all these heavy conversations. There is no door on the bedroom. All the windows are open screens. People are coming in and out of the house. Francis is having meetings in between our personal melodrama. The vice-president of United Artists is here. The sound editor has flown in from London. Tomita came from Tokyo to discuss the music. The picture editors arrived from San Francisco. Technicians are repairing the quadraphonic sound system in the bedroom.

March 20, Hidden Valley

I was on the Kurtz set today. Someone reminded me that the first day of shooting was March 20, one year ago. I have some footage of that day out at the salt farms in the river delta.

Tonight was the first big test shot of blowing up the compound. It was prepared all day and finally went about eight thirty in the evening. The temple ruins across the river were blown up. We were in bunkers on the main temple side. When the shot went, the explosions were so powerful they sucked the wind out of me at that distance. I jerked my camera, I'm sure. The fireworks and a number of specific effects were obscured by smoke. Stones and dirt rained down on the bunker. A high-speed camera was at another port in the bunker where I was. At the last minute the operator noticed I had my filter on when he was out checking his lens. He told me just in time for me to take it off. I would have lost the shot otherwise. I realized that having not shot for these past months, all the little automatic things I was in the habit of doing, I now forget.

Afterward we all went to the dining area for dinner. The night had been a real kick, but it wasn't like Do Long Bridge. I'm not sure why. Maybe everyone is just a little more tired now and we've seen powerful explosives before, or maybe it's because it's not 4:00 A.M. with the pressure of trying to get a big night shot before the sun comes up.

Dick White looked totally pale. He said a rock had hit the helicopter while he was flying the aerial camera. It missed the tail rotor by six inches. If it had hit the rotor, they would have gone down. As it is, the helicopter is grounded for repairs. Dick is not the nervous type. He went down nine times in Vietnam.

March 26, Hidden Valley

Francis has a houseboat docked at the set where he works and hangs out during the long preparations for a shot. We were sitting in there the other day. He was really depressed. He didn't want to go on. He wanted to just stop and go to bed and not get up. He started talking about how lonely he was. How essentially there are only two positions for most everybody to take with him. One is to kiss his ass, tell him he is great, and be paralyzed with admiration. The other is to resist him. That is, show him that no matter how rich and successful and talented he is, they are not impressed. Hardly anyone can just accept him, say, "That's great, and so what?" Francis was talking about how everything would be fine, everyone would like him if he failed with this film. Other filmmakers would say, "Well, it was just too tough to pull off, don't feel bad." Family and friends would sympathize and be caring. But if the film is a huge success, it will be one for other filmmakers to try to beat, people will want to shoot it down. More success and more money will make more resentments with family and friends.

Francis was talking about how everyone wants him to compromise; United Artists wants him to hurry up and just get done, never mind if the film will be better if he really does it the best he can. That I am willing for him to be uncompromising in his artistic life, but I want him to settle for less in his homelife and not live as well as he can imagine or have or do all the things that are possible.

March 26, Hidden Valley

Some strange things have happened lately. Several nights ago Francis was shooting on the main set at Kurtz Compound and the last shot of the evening was to be an insert inside the temple. For some reason he decided not to do it, but postpone it until the next day, a decision that wasn't logical because the camera was already in place and set. Ten minutes later a whole section of the stone ceiling of the temple caved in, shearing off the front of the camera. If anyone had been in there working, he would have been killed.

Several weeks ago when Marty Sheen had his heart attack, it seemed like the production would be stopped, but Francis held it together to keep the morale up. He started shooting around Marty in blind faith that he was young and strong and would recover and would be able to finish the picture. It went okay for a few days, then Francis collapsed, himself. That's when I came over. Now it looks like Marty is making a speedy recovery. He is out of the hospital and doing well. He expects to be able to work a few hours a day, starting in mid-April. In a way, the script is about confronting death and coming out the other side. Marty confronted it in real life. Imagine what that will do to his performance in the final scenes in the film.

Francis has said that he is the Willard character and when Marty was close to death Francis collapsed, too. He said he was as near death as he has ever experienced. He said he could see reality receding down a dark tunnel and he was totally scared that he couldn't get back.

March 28, Pagsanjan

8:30 A.M.—It is getting hot. I am looking out the window of Francis's houseboat docked at Kurtz Compound. Crews are building bunkers for cameras on Monkey Island and across the river. The river is so low that barges of materials are being pulled by men half swimming and walking through the water. They are preparing for tomorrow night's shot: another section of the temple blowing up.

I can see two women a bit downriver washing clothes in the shallow water. Another is spreading them out to dry on the short grass of the bank. There is an old man tending a small corn patch at the edge of the dense foliage. One of the biggest dangers is that the local people will sneak in for a close look during the big shots with explosives. Francis lives in terror of hurting someone. An extra got a second-degree burn during a shot two nights ago.

Boncas with waving tourists in bright polyester dresses, print shirts, sun hats and cameras continually paddle through the frame of what I see across the river.

There was just a call on the radio from Francis asking me to come upriver to where he is working in the gorge.

3:30 in the afternoon—I am back on the houseboat; I see that four camera bunkers have been completed and a fifth started. One is right where the women were drying their clothes. They folded the last stacks and carried them away on their heads.

A row of pants is still hanging on a wire between two poles in the corn patch.

Dean and Gary are in an outboard motorboat looking at the set from the different camera angles. They are across the river in front of two bunkers, calling instructions to their crew who are putting up banners. Four men are in the river positioning huge clumps of water lilies that will be seen in the shot.

This morning Sofia and I went in a bonca upriver to where the camera and PBR were. One of the Filipinos had caught a six-foot poisonous snake. It was still thrashing around in the shallow water. Francis got in our bonca and we were paddled up the rapids about a half hour to the first big waterfall. I hadn't been up there since I went with the kids last August. The high walls of the gorge cast cool shadows. We saw a two-foot lizard crawling along the rock wall.

Now and then Francis let Sofia call over the radio to Doug to see if they were ready for him yet. When they were about fifteen minutes from being ready, we turned around and headed back.

While the shot was being rehearsed, I sat in the shade on the bank. It was the first day that Martin's brother, Joe, was standing in for him. Sofia made mud pies at the river's edge. She asked me if she could "get worms that go in your feet and up your body and eat your food." Actually, I wasn't certain, and the water didn't look too clean, but she was already in it. I listened to one of the special effects men talking about his boat that could pull eight water-skiers. Dozens of boncas, mostly filled with Japanese tourists, continually paddled by.

———

Sofia is pretending to be a director. She is yelling "Action" at two guards on the dock. She is pretending she has a camera in her hands and is looking and focusing through her fingers.

———

I have an insect bite on the back of my hand. It is swollen and red and is really itching.

April 1, Pagsanjan

Yesterday Francis was shooting up in the gorge again. I went up and got a few shots. The location is upriver above some rapids, so the PBR they used was a mock-up, just the upper portion, floating on a raft of metal oil drums and boncas lashed together. Francis, Dean and the script clerk were in boncas being paddled alongside, watching the shot. I was being paddled slightly ahead of the crew so I could shoot back. My paddlers were an old man and his twelve-year-old son. They tried very hard to get me into the position I wanted. I had forgotten to bring my light meter, thinking I could get a reading from the production, but my lighting was different than theirs, so I had to guess at the exposures. The light had great contrasts late in the day. It was beautiful to look at but I don't know what I got on film.

When it got too dark to shoot, we came down to the Kurtz set to see the rehearsal of the evening shot: Monkey Island blowing up. We had waited all evening the night before and never gotten the shot because President Marcos was in the area and the production couldn't make contact with him to get permission to set off the explosions. If the explosions went off without warning he could think it was a rebel attack. Today Francis got a note of permission from him with regrets that he couldn't be reached last night. He said he was "in meditation." Someone said, "I'd like to know who she was."

Last night at midnight the special effects men went into the river and began removing explosives so there could be no accidents when the boat traffic started this morning.

The camera bunker where Francis was watching the rehearsal was the position by the bank across and downriver. I could smell the corn in the field next to us. Preparations continued for a long time. We sat in the dark waiting, listening to the radio. They were positioning the PBR. Set dressing began lighting the thousands and thousands of candles on the temple steps. Special effects were in position, Luciano was finishing the lighting, security men were fanning out through the surrounding area to make sure no local people were in danger. When the assistant director got the report that all the departments were ready, he sent the helicopter up with Enrico and the aerial camera. Vittorio was on his radio constantly, talking to the camera positions and to Luciano about the lighting. The helicopter got into position but had to go around again because there was a last-minute problem with lighting. Finally, everything was go. When the helicopter came into position again, the countdown began. Cameras rolled. "Action" was called. The PBR began to move, Monkey Island and the main temple and the dock were lit up. They flickered with about four thousand candles. Tall banners moved in little currents of air. The explosions started. Giant balls of fire, blasts of magnesium, white light and colored fireworks orchestrated together. I could feel the concussion of the explosions in my chest. They jolted me backwards. I could feel my camera move in spite of trying my hardest to hold it steady, sitting on the ground and bracing my knees against my chest. Finally a curtain of smoke obscured the set and Francis yelled, "Cut." My shot was of Francis silhouetted in front of the explosion. A big section of a fiberglass fake stone wall was on fire and out of control. I could hear Joe Lombardi yelling at his men to get the pump hoses in. We waited about a half hour for the fire to be controlled so we could cross the river.

When we went into the makeup department/dining room building, it was all decorated with flowers, some ice figures, candles on the tables and signs that said 200th Day of Shooting. There was a roast pig, prosciutto and melon, plus the regular dinner and the decorated cake. During dessert, a big silver-foil box was brought in and a girl jumped out in a bikini bottom with a lot of body-paint decorations. There were hoots and whistles. She had perfect red stars painted around her nipples. After the meal we went outside and Joe Lombardi gave Francis a button on a long cord to press. It set off a firework display that spelled out *Apocalypse Now*, 200th, Good Luck, Francis. There were rockets in the background and pinwheels. The whole thing was fun, but it looked like a peanut after the stuff set off for the evening shot.

April 6, Pagsanjan

Last night was the biggest explosion of all. It was the napalm run through the main temple. The special effects men said there had never been anything like it ever staged in the world before, outside a real war. I was in the bunker with the effects men, shooting a view through the two ports they looked out as they called the timing of each specific effect. The effects were orchestrated to go off seconds apart so there was a continuous chain of explosions, fire and changing color over a minute. The concussions were so powerful, a minute seemed like ages. At the end, people cheered and clapped. The sky looked like day all the way to Pagsanjan. The helicopter shot was perhaps the most spectacular of all.

I taped sound after it was over. Dean said on tape what I had been thinking, "God, you couldn't buy a ticket to a show like that anywhere in the world." Francis was saying, "There aren't too many places in the world you could even do it; they'd never let you in the United States. The environmentalists would kill you. But in a war, it's okay."

The special effects men were really excited and maybe a little sad that it was over.

April, A Few Days After Easter, Hidden Valley

Gio and Roman have come for Easter vacation. My back is itching. My sunburn is peeling. Last weekend we all went by helicopter to a remote island in the south. We camped out on a picture-postcard tropical island. It was uninhabited. There was a little fishing town on a finger of land a fifteen-minute boat ride away. People came from all around to see the helicopter and crowd around us. There were no tourists in the area. No hotels. The only Westerners were two Peace Corps workers who taught family planning and nutrition classes. The people were friendly, and curious, almost as if we were extraterrestrial. We bought fish and supplies in the town. On the island we were given crab, a squid and fish to eat with our watermelon and mangos. The island had white sand and a coral reef. We looked at amazing fish and sea life with a mask and snorkel. There were coconut palms, unusual birds and jungle vegetation. A few goats wandered about. A man who had been hunting gave us what he said was a pigeon. It had green and gray feathers and looked like a parrot. We roasted it over coconut charcoal. It tasted good.

A full moon rose over palm-covered hills. We slept on the beach, rolled in blankets. Several times in the night I woke up and saw fishermen looking at us and talking in Tagalog. Apparently, they pull up on the sand during the night and sort their catch. There were a lot of little fish along the water's edge in the morning and many flies.

Sunday it was Easter; we could hear the church bells in the town.

All day we swam. We explored the reef and little coves and lay in the sun. At the end of the day we packed up the helicopter and were back in Hidden Valley in about an hour and fifteen minutes. It takes three days by poor roads and little ferries to get there. The helicopter is the camper of the future.

Sofia wanted to know why the Easter Bunny had not come to the island. She talked about it a long while. Just why couldn't he come, "maybe he couldn't cross the water"? But she didn't believe it. When we got home, Sofia colored Easter eggs and laid out cake and drawings and flowers for the Easter Bunny. The next morning there was a letter from the Bunny saying he was sorry and he would come next Sunday. I went to Hong Kong the first of the week and fortunately I found leftover chocolate Easter eggs in the fancy pastry shop of the hotel.

April 15, Hidden Valley

I am sitting at a table on the porch of the boys' room. There are several cacao trees just outside the screened windows. The brown-red pods are hanging from the branches. The late-afternoon light is leaving the leaves. I got a letter saying the apple trees are in bloom in Napa. Barlow writes that there are black and white calves on the rolling green hills outside her windows in Petaluma and tulips are blooming on her sun porch. Dick came with the rumor that the production might close down due to Marty's condition. He said Francis had asked the production office to make reservations for us to go home in three or four days. I didn't realize how homesick I am.

A rumor here is like a rumor anywhere. There is about ten percent truth to it, maybe. Probably Francis is taking a stand to get Marty's doctor to give a definite date as to when he will be able to work. The work is dragging, with Francis spending a lot of time trying to get usable footage, using doubles and having to compromise.

I began thinking about the thousands of rumors that have circulated during the production. They are almost an art form. They are like that child's game where you tell something to one person and each person whispers it to the next in a circle. That is essentially what happens here, and everybody knows everybody in the circle. On location in Baler, the extras, who were staying in some vacated school-rooms, started putting the rumors on the blackboard. They called it "Rumor Control" so you could go in and read the rumor in its original form.

The rumors are mostly about who is screwing who, who is stealing what and changes in the production schedule. This morning I heard:

1. A secretly spent the weekend in Hong Kong with B and now might get fired.

2. B sleeps with his two Filipina maids in one double bed.
3. C is getting a kickback on all the plane tickets the company buys.
4. Tuesday the production is going to close down to wait for Marty.

April 19, Pagsanjan

This morning, Francis was anxious to get to the set. We got up early, woke up the pilot, got the kids going and went up to the helicopter. It wouldn't start. The battery was dead.

I was watching an ant move a chunk of pink and gold tinfoil through the grass at the edge of the landing pad while they tried to get the engine started. They got a tractor and a car and rigged jump cables. Finally we took off. There were several rainy spots as we flew. The kids stuck their hands out the window for a few seconds at a time, seeing how long they could stand it. The raindrops felt like prickly needles, like when your hand falls asleep.

We landed at the set on the grassy knoll, a little distance away, rather than on the central field, because there were banners and balloons that the wind from the helicopter landing would have blown away. There was a big sign that said Welcome Home, Marty. This is his first day back on the set. He arrived about an hour ago. He looks tan and terrific, like he just came back from Palm Beach. Francis put his ear on Marty's chest to check him out. He said he looked too good. The shot for today is a close-up, a pickup shot in the briefing scene where Marty is supposed to be really hung over and dissipated-looking.

The big news today is that Francis has decided to wrap May 15, finished or not. The rumors are really flying. Each department is flapping. Which scenes will be cut? The film has never kept to a date yet. Who will go home first? Who will stay and wrap?

—————

Francis and I have been arguing on and off for days. It has been very painful for both of us, and the kids have been witnessing the whole thing. Finally, yesterday afternoon, we were in the thick of an argument. Gina Lollobrigida came to the door, urgent, to see Francis. We were in the bedroom. We told Gio to ask her to go to the restaurant or something and come back in an hour or two. We went on arguing. I don't know how long. Finally Francis called Gio in and said what we have both been dreading so desperately: "We're getting a divorce; your mother and I aren't happy together and we're getting a divorce." Francis was sitting on the bed. I was at the table, crying with no tears left. Roman came in and said that Gina was waiting in the living room. I realized that the partition was open at the top and she could hear everything. Francis went out to talk to her. I went into the bathroom to cry. Finally, I put on my bathing suit and got Sofia and went to the warm mineral pool. Sofia was so happy, bubbly, full of life, showing me her newest tricks, swimming to the little waterfall on her back and pretending to shampoo her hair. The late-afternoon sun was just leaving the giant green leaves, my favorite red-stalked bamboo and huge ferns. Shadows were falling across the volcanic rocks. I noticed that I was feeling okay. Actually, I was feeling some kind of elation, just floating and looking around.

Francis and the boys came down the path. Francis looked grim. I could see he expected to find me weeping or cutting my wrists, or who knows what. We were swimming around. We began to realize that we both felt an enormous relief. We started acting silly, jumping around. Francis finally said, "Well, kids, how do you like us now that we're divorced?" Sofia said, "What is avorced?"

We took off our bathing suits. The boys started diving down and sticking their bare bottoms out of the water to moon us. We never all swam nude before. I've always been the responsible parent who doesn't know if it gives kids hang-ups or not.

Francis was telling me that when he talked to Gina he told her that his wife was in the other room crying and his production was $15 million over budget. She batted blue eyelids and asked him to help her, because Mrs. Marcos had promised to back her film and now wasn't coming through.

April 20, Pagsanjan

The helicopter is down. We went to the set by car. It's about an hour-and-a-half ride through intense green and yellow rice fields, dotted with little rural towns. We passed roadside stands selling pineapples, stalls selling carabao cheese, little hardware stores, bakeries, funeral parlors with open-air displays of shiny caskets, rice mills, candy stores with rows of penny candy in glass jars. There were people crowded into jeepneys, packed on tricycles, bicycles, old people sitting in the shade with white handkerchiefs on their heads, millions of little kids. You see no children in school uniforms now. It's summer vacation. The new term starts in June.

Today the rumor is that the production is scheduled to finish on May 21. A number of scenes have been cut. Everybody's spirits are up. They got nine setups yesterday. Marty had heart monitors on during the shots. Everything was okay. He said that coming back to work was the best medicine he could get.

April 21, Pagsanjan

Francis went to the houseboat during lunch today instead of eating. He wants to lose another ten pounds. Roman and I ate with the crew. We took our plates to a table and sat down across from Joe Lombardi. Joe started talking about the special effects business. How effects are very expensive. It doesn't matter if you are a big production or small, a bullet hit costs the same. I asked him how much one cost. He said, "Three dollars apiece." I started thinking about the machine guns strafing the bridge in Village II at Baler. There must have been thousands of hits and they did the shot over three or maybe four times, reloading the hits for each take. Joe was saying, "Guess what the cans of colored smoke cost?" I said I thought they cost about $4 or $5. He said $25. Thousands have been used at Kurtz Compound, especially. There were times when they used them by the hundreds, day after day. He said, "Just the 'willy petes' used at Kurtz cost a hundred dollars apiece." Two thousand gallons of gasoline went up in the napalm run. He said this is the biggest effects budget ever. I am curious to ask the accounting department what it all did cost, over more than a year of shooting. Joe said there won't be another show with effects this big for a long time. There are a couple of his crew who are in their mid-sixties. He let them set off the biggest phases of the explosions the last night at Kurtz. He said they'd never get an opportunity like that again in their lifetimes. One of his men, Jerry, worked on *Cleopatra*, *Sand Pebbles* and some of the biggest productions, but "nothing came close to this show in terms of effects."

April 25, Pagsanjan

Yesterday was Roman's birthday. His second in the Philippines. Three out of the last four years he has missed having a birthday party at home with his friends. Four years ago we were in Sicily for *Godfather II*. We had a birthday party for him and invited the crew. When the film wrapped, the presents were packed, but lost before they were shipped home. He still mentions those toys once in a while. Yesterday I asked the caterers to bring a birthday cake for him to the set at lunchtime. They only brought ten candles. So Roman cut two in half to make twelve. I had asked the wardrobe department to make him a shirt like the actors on the PBR crew wear. They made it with the river patrol patch and all. They found a small-size beret with the insignia, too. Roman liked it a lot. I got him some fake wounds from the makeup department and a survival kit from props.

I missed the whole thing. I was at the production office trying to get a reservation for Gio and Roman to return to San Francisco next week. The flight I wanted was booked. I hate to send them on a flight with an extra four-hour stop in Guam or somewhere. The trip is twenty hours as it is and strange enough. You leave Manila at 6:00 P.M. on a Tuesday, and are scheduled to arrive at 6:05 P.M. the same day, Tuesday, in San Francisco, crossing back over the international date line. Of course, Philippine Air Lines is rarely on time and you usually arrive about 2:00 A.M. Wednesday, very tired and grumpy.

When I got from the production office up to the set, I found out that where they were shooting was about an hour's boat ride away and there was no boat to get there. I waited around several hours with some of the propmen who were trying to get to the set also. The location was out of range of the radio. We couldn't even ask for a boat. Finally, I took a car back to the Rapids Hotel and drank iced tea and talked with Sue. We were talking about how it is to be in love with a person who is the center of focus and attention all the time. (She lives with the actor Sam Bottoms now.) How, when everyone around is telling the person he's such a fabulous genius, your reaction starts to be almost counter to that, as if to balance it. Sort of inadvertently withholding approval, and yet, you're the one whose approval the person trusts the most.

April 26, Hidden Valley

Saturday evening we jumped in the helicopter right after the last shot and flew to the island of Mr. Toda, the president of Philippine Air Lines. It was off the coast in the province of Zambales. We flew over Iba, where the typhoon hit the sets last year. The locations were nearly swallowed up by the jungle again, with barely a trace of our having been there. The last part of the flight over the water was beautiful. The sun had set. Hundreds of fishing boats were out. Their lights were on and, with the last of the daylight reflecting on the water, it looked like many little blisters on a skin of sea.

As we approached the island, the sound of our helicopter must have been the right frequency to speak to the bats. A giant cloud of big fruit bats rose over the runway. I could see that Dick was concerned. When we landed, he said that if one had hit the rotor we'd have been in trouble. We were taken to rooms in what they called the "bunkhouse." The rooms were native-hotel style with woven mat walls, ceiling fans and wooden-louvered windows. The kids were all in the room next to us and there seemed to be a number of guests in adjoining rooms. We showered and dressed for dinner and walked to the main house. It was big and open with huge verandas, bamboo floors, nipa roof, rattan furniture with thick, puffed-up pillows, parrots, native basket lamps, antique inlaid chests from Mindanao, a collection of exotic shells from the island's beach. There were six or eight guests speaking in Spanish. The kids were ushered to a big round table with the children of the other guests to have an early dinner. I wandered about, looking at the various facets of the interior. Seeing my interest, I was shown the giant double kitchen and some of the interior rooms. When the children finished eating, we were invited to attend Mass on the large porch on the side of the house facing the sea. Mass was said on Saturday night so that everyone could spend Sunday on the beach. I had a little trouble deciding whether it was polite to stand up and kneel down with everyone during the ceremony or if it was more appropriate to stay seated. The Mass was in English. Sofia was wide-eyed at the talk of drinking the blood of Jesus and partaking of the body of Christ. The priest was a Scottish-American who was a Jesuit and apparently a friend of the jet set. At dinner he was talking about the interior white leather upholstery of Mrs. Marcos's jet and how it wasn't being kept up very well.

Our host appeared just before the Mass began. He was a short man wearing a Chinese silk jacket. He escorted us to dinner on the lawn by the swimming pool. He was dieting, and only had a hamburger patty and no wine, while the rest of us stuffed ourselves from the big buffet table. Mr. Toda was full of lively stories about his travels, about a trip to China, about flying to all sorts of places in the world, about planes and boats, about a two-man submarine he had. He talked about planting mango trees on the island, then he dispatched someone to order mango juice from Manila and have it flown up in the morning. He talked about the island. Francis talked with him about buying jets, about buying an island. After dinner he showed us his private study, his Sony video recorder and giant bathtub.

The next morning we were served a big breakfast. A lovely, gray-haired hostess, house manager, who had greeted us when we arrived, now sat with us and told us about the island. She took us on a tour in a little open truck. We passed the nine-hole golf course, newly planted mango trees, coconut palms under cultivation, a lighthouse, an open field with what looked like a miniature housing development—there were rows and rows of four-foot-high nipa huts. We were told that each hut contained a fighting cock. Mr. Toda's son raises them. He brings week-old chicks from the United States. We passed cattle and sheep and more areas planted with mango trees. There were well-kept houses of employees, each with white coral stones lining their paths and flowering bougainvillea in neat pots. Our hostess said that each year she gives prizes to the house with the most flowers and the neatest yard. There are twenty-six families living on the island. Finally we arrived at the boathouse. Francis and the boys looked at everything. There were about twenty boats, all kinds; the two-man submarine was rusting slightly on its trailer. There were sailboats, ski boats, pedal boats, a landing craft and a Hovercraft. The beach was beautiful, with white sand and clear warm water. There was a big covered veranda with dressing rooms and a huge kitchen at the rear. The other guests had been at the beach for quite a while and had already been swimming. The priest was deep in a Scrabble game with a woman from Spain who had been in a Japanese prison camp in Shanghai during World War II. There was a soft-ice machine filled with pineapple juice. We served ourselves many glasses. We swam, Sofia played with the other children, Gio went sailing on a catamaran. Roman and I wandered up the beach finding starfish and shells. Francis swam out and got on board the catamaran with Gio. After a while everyone congregated on the veranda and lunch was served. At our table a man was talking about Philippine history. About how after World War II the Philippines had asked for independence from the United States and gotten it, but they resented the fact that the United States went to Japan and rehabilitated it. Now Japan is a rich world power and the Philippines, who had fought for the Americans against the Japanese, is a poor Third World nation catering to Japanese labor-class tourists.

Our host was not at lunch. Rumor was that he was with a beautiful woman in a private section of the house. As we departed, in the midafternoon, he drove up to the helicopter and said a warm good-bye and invited us to come back any weekend. We lifted off. It seemed like a long flight back to Pagsanjan.

Around seven in the evening we went to the big dining room of the hotel where Francis was the host of a cocktail party to thank all the local dignitaries and people who had helped the production. Francis gave a little speech, so did the governor of the province, the chief of police and various others. They said that the *Apocalypse* company had been good ambassadors. The millions of dollars they brought to the local economy were more help to them than any government economic aid program had ever been. They hoped that the film would be very successful so that we would come back and make more films there.

May 4, Manila

I am having lunch by myself in Manila. It is my forty-first birthday. I asked Delia to spend the day with me, but she couldn't leave the set. Yesterday the people who owned the property where they were shooting said it would cost another 50,000 pesos to stay five more days. Francis said no. They had already paid 10,000 pesos for two weeks. So, set dressing began removing the skull-pile set and special effects took out the arrow-attack rigging. Last night there was a settlement for 25,000 pesos. Today everyone is hustling to put the set back together.

May 5, Hidden Valley

When I got home from Manila yesterday evening, Francis had a surprise birthday party for me. He had flown his parents in from California. He had asked his father to compose a tango as a present. He hired a little orchestra to come to Hidden Valley. He invited Dean and the Italians. We took over the restaurant. Francis's mother and Alfredo's wife made pasta. After dinner, Francis's father conducted the orchestra as it played "Tango Eleanora." I danced with Francis and with Luciano and Alfredo. We dipped and whirled around the tiny floor in the hot night until we were all dripping with sweat. Sofia got up on top of the table with the birthday cake to help me blow out the candles.

May 11, Pagsanjan

Yesterday I went up on the hillside where the special effects men were getting ready to shoot off the arrow attack. They were hidden in little clearings, chopped out of the jungle, connected by paths cut through the foliage. It reminded me of a layout for Japanese gun emplacements in an old World War II movie. I set up my camera in a clearing that had a good view of the river. I wanted a shot with the effects men firing in the foreground and the arrows raining down on the PBR. I happened to be wearing red pants and a colored shirt which might be seen in the shot, so I borrowed a khaki shirt from the effects man, Jerry, and took my pants off. Jerry gave me a look. He is about sixty-five. Maybe I looked like a young chicken to him, or maybe it was the "director's wife" taking her pants down that did it. I stood in the bushes for the shot. There were ants crawling on me. It took a lot of effort to keep shooting during the whole action without stopping to brush the ants off.

I am sitting on the roof of the PBR. The production is waiting for the light to match the last shot. I can see a man in the river swimming along, pushing a rock in front of him. A fake boulder must have gotten loose during the last shot.

Sofia is sitting on Gani's lap. She is asking him why he doesn't wear a guard costume. Why he has his pistol in the back of his blue jeans. Why it is sticking out of his T-shirt. Why he doesn't have a holster.

I can hear Roger and Charlie talking close to me on the bank. Roger says that he's going to have a Bob's Big Boy hamburger as soon as he gets home. Charlie said he read that Americans ate forty billion hamburgers last year.

May 12, Pagsanjan

Today we flew over Kurtz Compound in the helicopter. Bulldozers have completely cleared the rubble from the explosions. The ground was covered with a kind of pinkish colored dust from the adobe blocks. There was nothing left of the set. I could see workmen preparing the soil to replant coconut palms down to the river's edge. In a year there will be no clue that the set was ever there.

May 13, Pagsanjan

We are on the PBR in the river. They are preparing for another take of Marty's close-up during the arrow attack. Propmen are in the water gathering up the arrows floating from the last shot. Francis is talking about going to Musso Frank's when he gets home and ordering a romaine lettuce salad with anchovy dressing.

May 17, Manila

Yesterday I didn't want to leave Hidden Valley. Sofia and I were all packed. I wanted to stay another day or two and just swim, walk by the big waterfall and sit on a rock and listen to all the insect noises. But I had already changed our departure once, said good-byes and not left. It seemed absurd to do it again. When we got to the airport I almost asked the driver to wait and make sure we got on the plane. But it was so hot, and we were an hour early, there was no logical reason that we wouldn't depart on schedule. When we got through the passport check and up to the check-in, I was told that the flight we were on had left. The time typed on our itinerary was an error. They were very sorry. We were taken to the airline office, where they phoned and fussed over us for an hour to get us on the already booked flight the next day. I tried to be an observer, watching what twist my life was taking, watching myself being checked into a hotel. Finally, Sofia and I were in a room. The hotel was one that was just being completed when we came to the Philippines last year. Now the decorator burnt-orange carpet had spots on it, the stitching on the quilted bedspread was missing in places. There was a candle in the bathroom which now I knew was not for mood lighting, but for when the electricity goes out. The toilet seat had a chip and there was a long black hair in the bathtub.

When Sofia and I went down to breakfast I asked the hotel receptionist what time the Philippine Village opened. She said 8:00 A.M. We got there about 10:00 and took a jeepney to the Mindanao section. There is a quite good folk art museum and several regional-style houses that sell baskets and handwoven things that I like. I went there last year on my birthday and really enjoyed it. Everything was closed; only one place was open that had junky shell jewelry. It was very hot. We walked to the next section where there were rice terraces and Ifugao huts. There was an old bare-breasted woman and some young girls weaving under the houses. There were little kids running around and chickens in baskets just like on the set. I could see up into some of the huts. One had a Samsonite suitcase stored in the rafters and a shelf with Modern Library books. Another had a baby sleeping on the floor and a row of plastic clothes bags filled to overflowing. Sofia was hot and thirsty and complaining.

June 16, San Francisco

Francis came home from the Philippines via Asia and Europe on a huge private jet. Dean, the Italians and some of the editors were on board. They cooked pasta, made espresso and watched videotapes of the footage as they traveled. Francis called me from Kuala Lumpur where they were refueling and waiting for permission to fly the next leg of the journey. They dropped off the Italians in Rome and went on to the south of France for the Cannes Film Festival. They flew to Paris and then to Madrid for the bullfights, then back to Paris, London and on to New York. It seemed very gala, but when Francis got home he was not all relaxed and cooled out and saying it was wonderful fun. He is jumpy and nervous. He is smoking a lot and is irritable. Maybe he is just scared. The shooting phase is over, and he doesn't know for sure if the footage will all cut together into a film that works.

June 22, San Francisco

Last night the dinner was all ready. The roast was roasting, the banana bread was baked, the table was set. Fred called and said Francis was going to have dinner at Vanessi's and continue his meeting with Mickey Rooney. Would I like to come? I went with Dean and Gio from the house in the Porsche Dean was driving. It was funny to be squeezed in on Gio's lap. Gio was an infant on my lap in the Porsche we used to have.

We waited by the front door at Vanessi's for our table. Mickey was greeting people who recognized him. He was *on* the whole evening, telling stories, doing parts, shaking hands with well-wishers over the wall of our booth. He was totally entertaining, his life and his art seemed to be one.

June 23, San Francisco

Yesterday, I went up to Francis's office for a few minutes. He was sitting at his new video editing machine, running the opening sequence of *Apocalypse Now*. There were images on three video screens that he dissolved together on the main monitor. It was amazing. Three layers of image. It was spatial. Francis says it changes the whole editing ball game. Pictures can be laid down layer upon layer, the way sound is edited. I got a rush, standing there, contemplating the possibilities.

July 20, Napa

I am sitting upstairs in the bedroom of this big Victorian house. It is completely empty. The furniture I ordered hasn't arrived yet. Francis, the children and I have been staying in the cottage, but today we can't be there because they are dressing it to use as a set for a montage of images of Kurtz's wife at home. The production is here in Napa to shoot inserts and pickup shots that weren't finished in the Philippines. Vans are arriving with equipment and props that were shipped back. The PBR is resting under a huge oak tree near the road. The helicopter is parked in the driveway. Vittorio, Enrico and Alfredo are down at the coach house assembling the camera and lighting equipment. Cases of props are being unpacked in the barn. Wardrobe is being hung on rods in the old cook's house. John La Sandra's men are putting up military tents in the meadow and building part of Kurtz's Compound. Cases of fake skulls and weathered totem poles are stacked in the grass.

I feel dislocated again. Things aren't where I expect them to be.

July, San Francisco

Francis is having a series of medical examinations. United Artists is taking out $15 million dollars' worth of life insurance. Francis says he is worth more dead than alive. He owes $14 million in production overages.

September 2, San Francisco

Francis was completely tuned out at the table last night and fell asleep right after dinner. We woke up early, about 5:30 this morning. Sofia, Roman and Chris were making noise and jumping around. They were all supposed to be sleeping together on Sofia's floor. Francis was real depressed. He has been working with Walter the last two days. Walter has been very candid. They have looked at a rough assembly of the footage. Francis says he feels that there is only about a twenty percent chance he can pull the film off.

Quite often people ask me what will happen in our lives if he doesn't.

September 20, Napa

Yesterday I was talking to Francis on the phone. He said he was in his office getting ready to meet with the editors. But all he could really focus on was his life. He said it was as if when he looked out of his left eye, he could see nothing but problems, and when he looked out of his right eye, his life looked perfect.

This morning I was telling Roman about the conversation. Roman said, "Why doesn't he just keep his left eye shut?"

September 22, Napa

Last week, Sofia said she wanted to go to a class after school with her best friend, Kristen. She said the class was "caterpillar kissing." I checked it out. The class was catechism. She went for the first time today. When she came home she said, "God is the father of everybody, so Kristen is my sister." She was very pleased. Later she said, "Katie is my sister too, but I hate her."

September 23, Napa

Barlow was just telling me about tarot cards. She said that they were based on court royalty of the day and the people of the land looked to the court and watched the behavior there. We were talking about how people in the media, like rock stars, movie people and TV personalities, are the royalty of today, and now everyone watches the goings-on of the members of that court. She was saying how, in a way, Francis is like the emperor. The emperor on the tarot card has only one eye.

October 1, Napa

I am sitting in the bleachers. St. Helena High has just completed a long pass for a touchdown. The announcer is saying, "There's a penalty on the play; personal foul against St. Helena." The ball is being brought back to the forty-six-yard line. The crowd is moaning. I am weeping. I have been breaking into tears off and on all evening. Nobody seems to notice. I have been watching the game on the field and replaying in my mind all the scenes of this last week with Francis. He told me some truths. I had been comfortable believing the lies. Now I am grieving over the death of my illusions. Disbelieving, then angry, then sad, then angry again, with an occasional flash of exhilaration and release from the tyranny of my blindness.

I am weeping again. When it gets too noticeable, I hold the program in front of my face. At the top it says St. Helena High School, Junior Varsity Football 1977. A little way down the page it says Number 20, Gio Coppola, Grade 9, height 5'7", weight 110 lbs., position: End.

I can hear "Hand off to Beltrami, picking up about four yards on the play." In my mind's eye I can see myself last week picking up the vase of flowers and throwing it. I can see it hit the wall and the glass spray out across the room toward Francis.

"Pass to Belts, good for two yards. One minute and thirty-eight seconds left in the first half."

October 8, Napa

I had thought that the making of *Apocalypse Now* was over. I was comfortable being home, starting a Zazen class, meeting once a week with friends to analyze dreams, making fig jam. I could see that Francis was in some deep conflict. We had long conversations about the themes of the film. We talked about opposites, about power and limits, good and evil, peace and violence. I told him about the Zen book which talks about mind and body not being two separate things and not being one thing, but being both two and one.

We talked about how the film was a parallel for the very things that Francis was living out this year. How he had been Willard setting off on his mission to make a film and how he had turned into Kurtz for a while. I thought when he resolved the conflicts within himself, he would see the end of the film clearly. I was busy getting the kids back to school, working on remodeling the house, cooking the fresh vegetables from the garden that all seemed to be ripe at the same time.

Two weeks ago, Francis was as miserable as I have ever seen him. I asked him to tell me about his conflicts, really tell me. He began to cry. He said he was in love with another woman. He said he loved her and he loved me, that we each represented a part of himself and he couldn't give up either. I listened to the person I love, in complete anguish and pain. Suddenly I could see the conflict for him was not about peace and violence. The conflict for him would be about romantic ideals and practical reality. A man who loves romance, loves illusion. He's a filmmaker, in the very business of creating illusion. And he loves his wife, he loves his children and fifteen years of that reality. I could see it so clearly. Then, the emotion rose up from my feet like a tide. It hit me in the chest and knocked me backward.

I saw myself pick up the vase of flowers and throw it. I heard the words pour out of my mouth. I saw myself go downstairs, and the fragments of white dishes hit the red kitchen walls. I was blind with rage. I was raging at my blindness.

October 9, Napa

This morning I woke up at 4:48 A.M. My eyes popped open. I couldn't sleep anymore. My mind ran through everything I've been thinking about. It was like a videotape, going forward and backward and replaying certain scenes. I began to see more and more of the parallels between the film and Francis's life. Willard's journey starts off in one context and, little by little, he goes farther upriver until he is in a very different place, almost without realizing the progression of changes that have brought him to that point. He reaches a place that is not like he expected or intended.

Francis is in that place within himself. A place he never intended to reach. A place of conflict, and he can't just go back down the river, because the journey has changed him.

I was watching from the point of view of the observer, not realizing that I was on the journey, too. Now I am at a place, I don't know quite how I got here. It feels strange and foreign. I can't go back to the way it was. Neither can Francis, neither can Willard, neither can the United States. It is fairly easy to be peaceful at Disneyland and violent in the front lines at war. The trick is to hold the peace and violence of our nature in the same place at the same time when the situation is not so clearly defined. It is fairly easy to be romantic where there aren't practical considerations; the trick is to be both romantic and practical with the same person. The trick is to be a whole human being, holding all the opposite aspects of ourselves in one dynamic balance. Ha.

October 10, Napa

If I tell the truth, we both strayed from our marriage, probably equally, each in our own way. Francis has gone to the extremes in the physical world, women, food, possessions, in an effort to feel complete. I have looked for that feeling of completeness in the nonphysical world. Zen, est, Esalen, meditation. Neither is better nor worse than the other. Both of us have been out of balance, not including our opposite aspects within ourselves.

Well, I feel like I got a great kick in the gut. It has jolted me awake, I have been in the real physical world, confronting a whole spectrum of emotions for perhaps the first time in many years. I had been lying to myself. I had been theorizing and spacy, critical, practical and responsible in my own way, but denying my guts, my emotions, my anger, my jealousy, denying my senses. I see myself, the spectator, the observer, like a camera, looking at my life from a distance, almost as if I were outside my body. Maybe I was. Right now, every inch of me is prickly with feeling. I am waking up.

October 12, Napa

The other day I had a fantasy about how I felt. I saw myself as a mummy, up at bat in a night baseball game. The spotlight was on me, but I could neither pick up the bat, nor see the other players in the darkness. I couldn't even see where the next ball was coming from. I knew it was about to be pitched.

Francis promised me he wouldn't go to see her. I just found out he is there.

It feels like the ball hit me right in the stomach.

October 14, Napa

Barlow just looked up "apocalypse" in the dictionary. One of the definitions was, "revelation of hidden knowledge."

October 16, Napa

I have always been waiting. Waiting for whatever project Francis is on so intensely to finish. As if then I will be able to breathe. Today I walked out into the garden; I could smell the fall. There was nothing to wait for. It was scary and exhilarating. I feel as though someone took the cast off and said walk! But I can't remember how.

Part of me has always believed that my prince, an artist, would make my life happen for me. Make me feel complete. Today I knew the waiting is over, my life is up to me.

I realized that I have always been waiting. Waiting to be old enough to drive, waiting to go away to college, waiting to fall in love, waiting to lose my virginity, waiting to finish college, waiting to get a job, waiting to get married, waiting to have a baby, waiting for Francis to get a chance to direct, waiting for him to finish his film, waiting for the next one, waiting to go on location, waiting to go home. Waiting for the rough cut, waiting for the fine cut. Waiting for the kids to start school. In recent years, time got more compressed, but it was basically the same. In the Philippines, I waited for the light to change, waited for the lunch break, waited for the mail.

October 21, San Francisco

When I started making notes, over a year ago, I tried to make them like photographs. I wanted to leave out the

---

adjectives, the judgments. Just make little snapshots that all together would give a picture of my experience. I was the camera, outside the events, just trying to record them. Now I find myself a participant.

I had a long, tearful conversation with Francis. He was calling from France. I was late getting back to Napa to meet Sofia's school bus. I stopped at a deli to get a quick sandwich. I am getting thin again. The only sandwich on the menu I thought I could swallow was chopped liver. I ordered one to go and took it to the car. I started the engine and got out the sandwich to eat on the way. The man had not cut it in half and it was too large to hold in one hand and drive. I tried to break it in half. It sort of tore, and a gob of chopped liver and mustard oozed onto my lap. I tried to scoop it up with the edge of the paper bag. Chopped liver got onto the steering wheel. It squeezed out between my fingers. I had no napkin. I reached in my purse for some Kleenex. Globules fell off my fingers onto my wallet, smeared across my checkbook. The Kleenex sort of melted into little rolls as I rubbed my hands.

October 24, Napa

I was driving down the freeway on my way to the Zen class. I was thinking about the chapter in the book about "right attitude." I was sitting up straight, trying to just be there, driving my car and the car driving me. I passed the marquees of a drive-in movie. There was a double bill: *Meat Cleaver Massacre* and *Cannibal Girls*.

216

November 4, Napa

I went to an Italian restaurant by myself for lunch. I sat on the terrace. The light was falling through the leaves, making patterns on the people. There was an attractive man and woman sitting at a table behind me. They were laughing together intimately. I imagined their sweet conversation. I wished I was in the flush of a romance that was new and uncomplicated. The terrace grew quiet, I could hear the couple talking. The woman's voice faded in and out . . . "I needed a lot of strokes I wasn't getting; that's when Brad came along. We went on this all-expense-paid trip to Hawaii; he was buying condominiums. Well, I never slept with anyone before who knew about it. There's this dynamite muscle in your rear end that with the right massage . . ."

November 7, Napa

I am looking out the window of the cottage. The fall leaves are blowing, tumbling and skipping along the paths by the pond. Yellow and rust colors mix with evergreen. The main house was supposed to be ready to move into September 1. We are still waiting. I have been in this same point so many times before in my life. We were in a little two-bedroom apartment during the shooting of *Godfather I* in New York, the two boys in one room and Francis and I and our new baby, Sofia, in the other. During *Godfather II* we were in a small bungalow for six months on the set at Lake Tahoe. And now we are here in this two-bedroom cottage, squeezed in and temporary, with three children in one room, plus two parrots we inherited from the film. They screech at sunrise. I have been in this same situation so many times. There has been extraordinary physical beauty outside, all around me, and cramped disorder inside where we are living.

November 8, Napa

I have just heard that United Artists has agreed to postpone the opening of the film from May to next October. It will be an enormous relief for everybody working on it. Best for Francis.

November 10, Napa

The house here and the house in San Francisco are beautiful old Victorian mansions. I have tried to make decorating choices that would enhance the architecture, make it comfortable and livable, but always retain its architectural integrity.

I am not a Victorian.

A few days ago I got a vision of a house that I would feel at home in. It was made of eucalyptus, glass and adobe. A contemporary structure in a natural setting. I would have to build it. I walked up by the old water tank today, looking for a site.

Through the years, Francis and I have argued over and over again about our house. He has said all he ever really wanted from me was to make him a home. Once, in a crazy argument in the Philippines, he told me that he would spend a million dollars, if necessary, to find a woman who wanted to make a home, cook and have lots of babies. I could never tell the truth, even to myself, because I thought it would be the end of my marriage. I am not a homemaker. I have always wanted to be a working person. But the kind of work I have done over the years hasn't earned any money, so it looks like I am playing and lazy.

Right now I am feeling a giant relief. I am off the hook. The other woman in Francis's life is not the ultimate home-maker either; she is not dying to step in and take over the mansion.

November 14, San Francisco

We went to Francis's new sound mixing studio to hear some tests. A large black-and-white work print of *Apocalypse Now* filled the screen at the end of the room. There was a giant console with three technicians operating huge control panels. It looked like part of a *Star Wars* set. We sat in the darkness watching Do Long Bridge footage go fast backward, and then forward with some of the sound tracks. Francis was whispering to me about having seen a new doctor and learning that he has had a real breakdown that can be treated. Then we heard machine-gun fire right behind us and jets streaking overhead, and Francis talked to the man on his right about how this was the first true quadraphonic movie sound studio in the world.

November 16, Flight to Washington, D.C.

I am sitting on an airplane with the hors d'oeuvres plate on the folding table in front of me. Crab legs, cocktail sauce, mayonnaise, lettuce leaf, macadamia nuts, lemon wedge, parsley, a fork, paper napkin and a glass of water with ice cubes, all lit from the side window like a little still life. Francis is next to me. George Lucas is leaning over the seat in front of him. Steve Spielberg is across the aisle. Between them they hold the top three film grosses of all time. *Jaws* is number one. George just said that *Star Wars* will be number one at 7:05 next Saturday night. *Godfather* is number three. Between them, their films have grossed over a billion dollars. Steve calls them the billion boys. They are talking about the depression they felt after a big success. All their drive and focus to get the big hit, the dream of their life. They are talking about the jolt of actually doing it. Steve is saying that after *Jaws* opened he wanted to get away, he went around the world, there was no place but India and Russia where there weren't *Jaws* billboards and T-shirts.

Francis is talking about using success to stretch the bounds of filmmaking. Stretch the form, make the films you want, make a forty-minute film, a six-minute film. To be able to say, "I'll never make a picture again as successful as *Jaws*, *Star Wars*, or *Godfather*." And make the films you really want to make.

Steve wants to do a live TV show. Francis is saying, "Do a daytime soap if you want to. Take a chance, be risky." George said, "You, too, Francis."

Francis replied, "Yes, but I no longer have the financial base." George said, "Ah, come on, you'll always have the money." Francis is saying, "You just have to make something beautiful; you can't worry about if anybody will see it. You can distribute it. Success is a drug. It's like a woman: if you chase it, you won't get it." George said, "Success is a drudge, like chasing girls."

November 17, Washington, D.C.

Last night we went to the reception at the White House. We waited in a receiving line to meet the President and Mrs. Carter. They didn't know what Francis and George had to do with the movie business. They recognized the movie stars and Andy Warhol. The White House was smaller and more tasteful than I expected. The Red Room was almost intimate. The flowers were beautiful, like fresh garden bouquets. It wasn't stuffy elegant, like places I've been to in Europe.

We had wanted to bring Gio and Roman with us. We rented them tuxedos and asked for permission right up to the last minute. They were not invited. We saw two kids running around among the guests. Francis was annoyed that other people got to bring their children. When we got closer, we saw that it was Amy Carter and a friend. Mark Hamill gave her a storm trooper mask from *Star Wars*.

Later, at dinner, in the Kennedy Center, someone was passing around a White House ashtray she'd swiped. Henry Kissinger, Elizabeth Taylor, Charlton Heston, all the famous people who passed our table, didn't look as real in life as they do on TV.

It's as if the core of me is trying to cut through the illusion and look at the structure.

Francis wants to cover over the seams and wrinkles of life and maintain the illusion. That is the basis of filmmaking.

We are staying at the Watergate Hotel. We ordered room service breakfast. It took a long time. After the waiter left, we realized there weren't enough napkins and silverware. We shared knives; I stirred my coffee with my egg spoon. Roman wiped his mouth on the sleeve of his plaid shirt.

George was talking about film discs and cassettes. How filmmaking will be more focused on specific scenes, less concerned with the linear story. People will put on a video disc and play just the love scene or the chase scene or the sad scene for a certain emotional mood effect, like we put on certain music to feel a certain way. We talked about the film format changing.

The food was awful, the conversation was filling.

November 18, Washington, D.C.

A photographer has just called Francis downstairs to have his picture taken with George Lucas and Steve Spielberg as the three hotshot directors. A few years ago, Francis had his picture taken with Peter Bogdanovich and Billy Friedkin as the three hotshot directors.

November 20, New York City

I am in New York. Gio was sick in the night. This morning he got in my bed and fell asleep. When the maid came in and saw a young man in my bed, she hurried out. I was talking to Francis on the phone. He was telling me that he is trying to let go of his outdated belief systems. Then he remembered that Willard is this guy whose belief systems no longer work.

November 21, New York City

I just came in from a movie and called Francis to say good night. I could hear a party going on in the background. He said that the huge palm tree in the backyard had fallen on the house. It went through the roof, Gio's room and the breakfast room, landing on his chair. He had just gotten up a few minutes before. He said there had been no warning sound; it fell like a bomb. He called up some people to come over for a survival party.

November 26, San Francisco

I have just spent a week in New York with the boys. I see how hard it is to initiate all the action. I am so used to Francis doing it for me. It was hard to get moving. I was sad on Thanksgiving, not to be together with Francis and Sofia, making a traditional dinner.

The boys and I went to the Macy's parade. They climbed up a wall at a subway entrance and pulled me up above the crowd lining the street to see. We went to the zoo. We got dressed up to eat an afternoon dinner at the Russian Tea Room, blini and red caviar and shashlik. We went ice skating. I haven't been for about twenty-five years. It was exhilarating to finally get off the wall and make it around the rink without holding on. We went to the theater at night.

224

The first two theater performances we went to, our seats weren't very good. I didn't know that someone had to call and say Mrs. FFC would like house seats. I didn't know where to eat. I have always been taken. Taxi drivers didn't give me the right change. I'm not sure if I overtipped or undertipped at the hotel. By the end of the week I felt I just made it. Having fun was a real effort.

Late November, San Francisco

We watched the last section of *Godfather II* on TV. Bobby Duvall was there. Every time one of Bobby's scenes came on, there was a lot of hooting "Mighty moment" and Duvall laugh imitations. I missed most of my favorite scene of his with Michael Gazzo by the prison fence.

November 27, San Francisco

Last night we ran the home movies I took in Hidden Valley. We hadn't seen them before. There was no sound track, the kids kept up a running commentary, telling us things like when Roman was going to flash his bare bottom at the camera. We were downstairs in the screening room. When the films were finished, Francis asked the kids to leave so he could show Fellini's 8½ to me, alone. He had seen it a few days before and wanted me to see how it paralleled his own life. God, what a movie! It was like an autobiography of Francis. Even the fantasies were the same. The dialogue between the husband and wife was word for word things Francis and I have said to each other. By the end I was sobbing. Francis was asleep.

November 28, San Francisco

I was talking to Fred about Carroll Ballard. Fred was saying that Carroll was having a hard time directing *Black Stallion*. He wasn't directing a fiction film with the same assurance that he did his documentaries. I understood immediately. The whole idea in documentary filmmaking is to watch what is happening and catch some moments on film as they pass by. Fiction filmmaking is about making things happen, shooting them over and over until they happen the way you want. The process is reversed.

December 13, Napa

Last night Francis said he was angry with everyone, especially everyone he loves. Only Roman was all right. The circle of people who make him happy has shrunk to one small mirror image. It's down to Francis being the only one left who can make him happy.

That's the ball game.

December 19, Napa

The film production was in the forefront of my life for so long, it is still very much going on, having its dramatic moments, but it is out of focus for me. It is at a distance. I heard that one of the editors stole the whole ending of the film, reels and reels of the print, and sent letters full of ashes to Francis every day for a week. George Lucas said to me, "God, you could make your movie about that."

December 29, Napa

I talked to several people on the phone today. I realized that lots of people know about my personal life. I have always tried to be a private person, not indulge in the gossip swirling around me. Now I find that it is my personal life that is the hot gossip. As if what we try to avoid we seem to meet.

People give me advice: "What you need right now, Ellie, is a great lover." Or, "Ellie, just hang in there, you know this is just Francis's way to avoid cutting the film. He makes a smoke-screen crisis. Remember during the editing of *The Conversation*, he was already into a production crisis on *Godfather II*, and during the editing of *Godfather II*, he got into the *City* magazine crisis. He always does something to prevent himself from being able to work on the first cut."

I can sort of understand that. Perhaps he can only really give his vision to the editing after there is a first cut and he can see it. But the contradiction lies in the fact that this film is so much his vision that the editors can hardly assemble it without his direction.

Out of my window are acres of vineyards, thick patches of yellow mustard blossoms among the rows of bare vines, blue-purple hills, slate sky, flocks of birds that rise in occasional clouds. The big fig tree looks old and small without its leaves. I am in this Victorian house, like a queen alone in her castle. The children are skiing, Francis is in New York receiving an honorary doctorate.

I was thinking about Jackie Kennedy in the White House. How she had to smile and shake hands, go where the Secret Service directed her, be a proper First Lady. Then, after she became a widow, she became visible, the center of international attention. She came into her own, in a way, only after her husband's death. There is part of me that has been waiting for Francis to leave me, or die, so that I can get my life the way I want it. I wonder if I have the guts to get it the way I want it with him in it.

December 30, Napa

I was looking at the pomegranate tree by the pond. There are still some fat pomegranates hanging on the bare branches. They are cracking open with smiling rows of dark red teeth.

All along I have been talking about Francis's conflicts, mirroring the conflicts of Willard. The contradictions of the peace-loving U.S.A. making a bloody war. I've been standing back, as if looking through a wide-angle lens, seeing the big picture. Now I have found myself with a close-up lens. It brings into focus *my* contradictions. I am laughing and crying my heart out. How I thought I was the innocent bystander, just recording some snapshots about the making of *Apocalypse*, as if it didn't pertain to me.

I had a belief system that took the world literally. I chose to only see the rational, the literal, and deny the illusion. I believed Francis's words literally. Just like Kay in the last scene of *The Godfather*. All of the evidence tells her that her husband has had people killed, and when she asks him, he says no, and she believes his words. All the evidence through the years, the little presents, notes, things I would find in Francis's pockets after a trip, the pin sent to him in the Philippines that he wore on his hat as a good luck charm. And when I would ask, I would hear, "Ellie, she is a friend, she has been a big help to me. Please be nice to her. She feels that you resent her because she once had a crush on me. She is no threat to you." I believed the words, I denied the evidence. I didn't want to see the truth. Now my guts ache, but I feel exhilarated. I am emerging from my tunnel vision. I am in a clearing where I can see more, see the literal and the illusion both at the same time. I am humiliated that my blindness was so obvious, so corny. While I was off taking hip consciousness-raising trips, enlightenment was right there in the "Dear Abby" column. There is a chapter in Gail Sheehy's book *Passages* on men's life patterns that describes Francis to a T. I'm right there, listed as the "utilitarian wife," and there is also the "adoring young protégée." My whole personal, gut-wrenching drama is just a common statistic in a $2.50 popular paperback book. It gets me right down out of the clouds.

PART THREE

1978

January 3, San Francisco

Last night we got in bed, and Francis talked through *Apocalypse Now*. He said making the film work was like trying to shoot a basket over your shoulder while you were standing sideways. He had the ball and he knew where the basket was, but he didn't know if he could get the ball in. He described how each sequence of the film evolved to the next and the style changed, transformed, from scene to scene, so the audience sort of goes along on the trip by accepting each new sequence. He was talking about how the editors have to cut each sequence in the style appropriate to it, rather than to a consistent, overall style.

I remember, sometime in the spring of 1976 out in the Philippines, Francis said that the film would be won or lost in the style. I thought he meant by the film being in CinemaScope with Vittorio's lyric photography, and a certain kind of acting. Maybe he did mean that, then. His vision has evolved. Francis talked about the first two-thirds of the film with clarity. He got bogged down in the ending. He said it was as though he could see the hoop, but the ball was rolling around on the rim.

Sofia started crying in the hall outside the bedroom. I got up and fixed her a scrambled egg and a bagel and put her back in bed. She said she was allergic to sleeping alone and couldn't she please sleep with me?

January 9, Napa

The other day I was up in Francis's office. He was putting Marlon's monologue up on the video monitor and talking about Kurtz being clear and lucid and totally mad at the same time. As he talked, it was a description of the state he was in during the last months in the Philippines. It seemed to me that Francis, metaphorically, lived every foot of the film he shot.

The editors left and Francis put on a tape of the Baler battle that he had worked on the day before. I had seen the footage in rushes and rough assembly and said, "Very impressive, it's going to be great." That's very different than seeing it and *it is* great. The emotion hit me in the chest; all the hopes, the fears suddenly escalated, became real instead of speculation. I drove to Napa. I tried to concentrate on the green rolling hills, the black and white cows, a blue van slicing the green horizon, stripes of yellow mustard between the rows of bare black grapevines. I couldn't.

January 16, Napa

A few weeks ago, the helicopter we used every day in the Philippines had an accident as it was getting ready to lift off. The rotor came through the cockpit. The pilots were rather short. Dick told me if he and Francis had been flying it, the rotor would have sliced their heads off.

The morning paper brings news that there has been a helicopter accident in Pagsanjan. A pilot, a film director and two others were killed while they were looking for locations right where we flew every day for months. One of the passengers was our production caterer. I remember how pleased he was with the dinner he served the night of the two hundredth day of shooting, the nude girl he sprung out of the silver aluminum foil box and the turkeys he got for Thanksgiving by conning some guys into buying them illegally at the American PX.

February 9, Napa

I have been crying all morning. Another layer of blindness is dying. I am grieving. When will it be over? I didn't record the twists and turns of the past months. As if I couldn't bear to look that closely, couldn't bear to expose my bumbling steps. I always wanted to be above the melodrama that rules the lives of others. So, here I am, sputtering, gulping, thrashing, flailing in a sea of emotion. I never learned to swim.

The tarot cards describe life's journey. At the halfway point, the seeker meets his shadow side. All the aspects he dislikes in others, whatever he thinks he is not, is discovered to be his own, unclaimed, shadow side.

February 13, Napa

Saturday night Francis was lying on the couch talking about some incident in the Philippines. I remembered I had a note about whatever it was and went to get my binder. When I got back he was dozing. I started to read; he woke up. I have never read my notes to Francis because he is a writer and I am not. I was afraid of his judgment. I read to him till nearly two in the morning.

February 14, Napa

Francis called me this evening. He said he got the valentine I sent him. He said he didn't believe in valentines but that he wanted me to know that my notes were really good, that he always knew that I had talent.

He said he is really getting scared.

He said he had been working very long hours. He is screening an assembly of the film in ten days.

February 17, Napa

I just called the house in San Francisco. Men were there cleaning the projectors, getting everything ready for the screening this week. Everybody will be working through the weekend. I am here in Napa. Out the window the orange tree is loaded with fruit, daffodils are blooming by the pond, the iris are budding, the tulip tree is covered with blossoms that look like egret feathers. All around me there is incredible beauty. Inside, a wave of sadness is taking its course. I am not part of the excitement. Francis wants to keep his focus on his work. Our personal life is postponed. I must not make any emotional waves, not interrupt the preparations for the first screening of the complete assembly of *Apocalypse Now*.

When Francis comes this weekend, I will ask him how the cut is going. How many minutes he was able to cut out of the ending sequence, about the narration. I will say, Don't be scared. Remember those guys that jumped out of the windows when the stock market crashed? They thought they were their money. You are not your movie. If people think it is great, you are not God. If people think it stinks, you are not a fool. You are a human being who gave it everything you had. You didn't spare anything, or anybody, including yourself. There is no more courageous act than that.

February 18, Napa

I have just signed my name thirty-seven times. A few signatures were on corporate minutes, the rest pertained to loans.

February 19, Napa

Victorian bedrooms have no closets. Last fall I got a French country antique armoire and a headboard that went with it, then a chest by the bed and a desk for the telephone and an old English table and two chairs by the window.

The other day I took all the furniture out. I put the bed in the bay window without the headboard, just lots of pillows. I got some bright French fabric with flowers and birds and made a spread. I painted one wall Chinese red. I pushpinned a purple silk obi the length of the wall, with some apple-green, Japanese-patterned paper, Chinese paper cuts of bright-colored opera masks and a round embroidery. I put a blue and white Japanese fabric on the coral wall behind the bathtub and an antique batik on the wall by the shower. All pushpinned to the Victorian walls, all changeable in minutes.

I feel a huge relief. As though I can breathe. Now there is a big expanse of soft blue carpet to lie on in front of the fireplace. From the bed I can see the moon in gnarled branches of the oak tree, the sunrise over the vineyard and misty hills. There is only a bed, a lamp and two bushy plants in the room. My books are on a tray under the bed. When the gardener came in to water the houseplants, he said, "Gee, your bedroom is much more romantic."

February 20, Napa

Francis was here yesterday. It was sad and happy. There were moments that I could stay in the present and enjoy being with him, enjoy being in his arms, enjoy the light falling on his hair. There were moments when I cried and told him how hurt I felt. Banished to this paradise, such beauty around me and him not here.

A tired, pale shell of the vibrant person I remember visits one afternoon and evening a week now. I am so angry with myself when I slip into feeling rejected. He feels guilty and more miserable. He said he fainted Saturday night. He has been working all day and all evening this week, preparing the assembly. He goes from one editor to the next. He said that he feels that seeing the film completed is going to clarify and complete something within himself, and, until he completes the film, he is in a personal chaos. He is shocked at how different he is than he used to be. He doesn't recognize himself. He can't divert himself with any of his previous diversions. He can't throw a party, listen to music, go to a movie, read a book, he can't get interested in a jet plane or the new mixing studio, or building a winery. He doesn't care whether the house is this way or that way, he says he has no opinion.

I try to be understanding, I try to be patient and let time take its course. Let Francis find himself. I ache for him and I ache for myself. I ache for the children and everyone intertwined in his life. The man, the father, the director, the employer, is not well.

February 21, Napa

I haven't used the I Ching for a year. Last night I consulted it. I got number 39, "Difficulty." It said:

A conflict has arisen between you and friend over something specific, something heretofore outside your relationship. This could be a third person to whom you each react differently . . . which is causing tension and contention. Obviously some conflict was bound to appear sooner or later, about one thing or another. Instead of trying to overcome the specific difficulty by compromise or by one of you assuming authority in the matter (such slapdash solutions can cause spitefulness on one part and regrets on the other), ignore the difficulty for a while; withdraw from it. Return to your convivial state before the difficulty appeared. Of course you both will remain conscious of the difficulty. But the love and pleasure and time you share will encompass and overcome the latent difficulty which you also share. When it arises naturally again out of your lives together, you can meet it together and react spontaneously as a couple.

February 22, Napa

I had lunch on the front porch. Patterns of strong sunlight and deep shade painted the garden. Shadows from the wicker furniture cast drawings on the porch. The air was fresh, carrying new scents of spring. The food on my plate grew cold without my realizing it. The day was delicious.

February 23, Napa

Yesterday I was in San Francisco. I called Francis around one to make plans to meet in the city for dinner. He said he had just gotten an idea about a twist for the ending. Instead of Willard killing Kurtz and calling in the air strike, he was going to try it where Willard gets double-crossed. The air strike which was supposed to be his defense would be sent in to kill him, too. He was real excited. He said to call back later in the afternoon to make our plans.

I had lunch, I did some shopping and waited around. I called back around four. He said he had everyone in there working and why didn't I just go back to Napa and he would come there in the evening when he got the editors all lined up with the new changes?

I got on the freeway, heading north. I felt a rush of emotion. I knew I would go home and wait, and he wouldn't come. I got more and more angry thinking about how my life is caught in so many moments of waiting. I drove to Carol's house instead of going home. She wasn't feeling well, she was lying in bed. There was a long bright rectangle of late-afternoon light on the wall behind her head. It framed a section of Peruvian textile and a piece of her valentine red pillow. We watched the sun set beyond the green fields and fingers of water and blue-purple hills outside her window. We talked about waiting. How women have historically been the ones who waited. She said that waiting has given women time to reflect, look inward.

We did a spread of tarot cards on the bed. The cards told me that waiting has two voices in me. One voice says, "Ellie, you're missing out. Get your life going. You're a fool to allow yourself to be put into the position of waiting for Francis. Make your own life. You only live once. Don't wait for anything or anybody."

The other voice in me says, "Ellie, when you are quiet, when you are waiting, not doing anything, that's when you get your best information. That's when you hear things, that's when you see things."

February 24, Napa

Francis came Sunday at noon and left Monday morning. I try to tell myself that at long last I have time to be by myself. Time I have always wanted. Time to spend long hours with my books and my typewriter. I always wanted to gain that time myself, by my needs' being considered by those around me. It feels as though I have gained the time, but through loss.

There is time and space between us. Neither of us feels the marriage is over. We can't go back to the way it was. The shape of the future isn't visible yet.

6:00 P.M.—Francis just called. He said he had seen the film up to the end. He was excited about how well it was working up to Kurtz Compound. He realized that the ending sequence didn't have to be so long, the rest of the film carried. He said the last sequence couldn't happen the way he'd planned. He'd have to dream up something new. Let go of his preconceptions. He thought he'd go for a walk, something to take his mind in a different direction so some new ideas could pop in from left field.

He said he had been working on the video editing machine by himself till four or five this morning. He said it was just like writing. Now the editors were trying to conform the film to the ideas he got from working with the videotapes.

February 25, Napa

The other night I went out on a date. He picked me up, he helped me on with my jacket, he opened the car door. At the restaurant he asked me what kind of beer I liked. I was conscious of my layers of unfamiliar feelings. When the Chinese waiter brought the check, he had neatly added it up and divided by two, circling two equal totals.

February 27, Napa

We took a tray with sangría out to the garden. Francis was pouring and Walter said, "Go hot, son." One of Colonel Kilgore's lines. Walter talked about how editing is like brainwashing. You sit in a darkened room day after day and hear the same dialogue over and over again. After a while you start using the party line. Walter said that the editors on *Star Wars* started saying, "Here they come," as an answer for anything.

Francis was feeling much calmer this weekend. He had the first screening with an audience the end of last week and got a very positive response. He was making changes in the reels right up to the last minute. The screening started an hour and a half late, but the men from United Artists, the editors and the other people who saw it confirmed that there *is* a film there.

I found a note in Francis's coat pocket. It said, "Incredible in its accomplishment as it stands and its potential to grow greater in the next weeks. A great honor and challenge to be part of it."

February 28, Napa

Francis and Roman and I were on the porch talking about the helicopter footage shot in Baler. Roman had gone up in one of the Hueys during shooting. Francis was recalling directing the helicopters from the command ship. How he had been so frustrated when they didn't follow his directions and fly the shots the way he wanted. He said he found out later that one of the pilots was sniffing heroin.

February 29, Napa

Francis said the first time he ever thought about being a film director was when he was fourteen. He was in the kitchen with his brother Augie and his wife. They were dancing around doing scenes from a romantic movie. Francis looked through his fingers pretending he was operating a camera, following their action.

March 1, Napa

When Francis was here on Sunday, I whined and cried and said all the things I hate myself for saying. I apologized and I hated myself for apologizing. I couldn't sleep Sunday night. I was so mad at myself for not being able to just enjoy the good moments.

Monday I was tired and grumpy when Francis left to go back to S.F. At noon I got in the car and drove to Petaluma to meet with Carol and Barlow and study the tarot. It was a spring day. I took photographs in my mind's eye. Sheep on a green hill with a perfect line of palm trees behind, black and white cows in front of a new housing development, a line of yellow mustard blossoms defining a property line. I promised myself I would bring my camera next week, but I knew my slides wouldn't be as good.

When I got to Barlow's house, I sat down in the kitchen and hastily turned to the chapter for this week on the card called the Tower. There was a picture of a stone tower being struck by lightning, splitting open with flames coming out of the windows. It said, "The Tower suggests the destruction of an outdated philosophy which is unable to adapt to new conditions. As the human mind develops it easily absorbs new ideas and concepts, using them to build a mental framework which will serve it as a guide during its life. But as the mind matures its principles tend to harden and gradually become fixed, thus it loses contact with the dynamism of reality."

As the afternoon wore on, something in me shifted, as if the glacier of my rigid thinking had finally cracked. I began to understand how I had built this structure, this belief system about marriage, starting from when I was a little girl. It hadn't adapted through the years, hadn't remained flexible and finally just cracked open. I started to lighten up; driving home in the evening, in my mind's eye, I could see all of the stones of my beliefs, gray boulders, lying on the ground around my feet. I began to change from feeling loss and pain, to feeling exhilarated about building something new.

March 5, Napa

Five days have passed. I keep looking out of the corner of my eye to see if my exhilaration is going away. It is still here.

March 13, Napa

Francis is tough. Part of him is still fighting to hang on to his old belief systems. He knows they are outdated and won't work for the next phase of his life, but they are familiar. He was raised on them and he wishes he could go back to a familiar, comfortable place in the past. At the same time he knows he can't. He is angry and sad. This weekend I saw the beginnings of a shift in him. We were driving along in the car with the kids. He started to sing. I was startled to realize how long it has been since I heard him sing. He began talking about his next project. Signs of change.

For me, that big, two-headed stone temple at Kurtz Compound represented marriage. The basic structure of beliefs that my life was based on. It exploded. I wept and ached and tried to put back the stones, hold up the walls and patch it together as it crumbled. Finally I gave up. I feel as though I am back on the river. The temple is smoldering in the background but I am floating on my back,

looking at the sky and the foliage. I don't know where the
river is taking me, I don't know what the next moment or
day of my life is going to be like. I can't imagine where I
will be or what my life will be like six months or a year from
now. It is scary, but mostly I am excited and curious to see
what unfolds.

March 18, Napa

We were sitting on the front porch talking about filmmaking being like a metaphor for living. We were talking about
editing. Francis said, "I am willing to sacrifice my best
scene to make the film better . . . anything . . . I can always put it back. That's the difference with life, you can't
put it back."

March 26, Napa

We have been talking about how the longer you remain in
a state of ambiguity, the more change can take place. We
have this urge to define things, make them definite, fix

248

them so we know what they are and can deal with them. Francis was talking about wanting to get the film cut, finished; yet the longer he can stand the pressure of not knowing the ending, not defining it, the more it can evolve. The same is true of our marriage. I go back and forth from wanting it defined, crying out, is it on or is it off, what is the structure of it, what are the perimeters, to being excited by the lack of definition and the potential for letting it evolve into whatever it is going to be. Then I cry again for form and definition, some structure to cling to. Perhaps I only want a definition so that I can rebel against something tangible as has been my habit.

April 1, Bolinas

There was a minus tide today and we all came to Walter's house to go clamming. I was late coming from Napa with the kids. The clam beds had too many diggers by the time we got there so Carroll Ballard, Gio, Roman and I and some of the kids walked about a mile down the beach to a point where there is a long reef. We went out on it to get mussels. There was no one there. It is odd that people here don't go for mussels. They are relished all around the Mediterranean. We went out where the waves were breaking. We passed tide pools with starfish, sea urchins and crabs. We could see seals sunning on the rocks farther out and more swimming just offshore. We pulled mussels off the rocks, and when the bucket was nearly filled, Francis caught up with us. He was barefoot, walking uncomfortably through the water and over the rough reef, carrying his leather loafers in his hand. He had come from San Francisco. He had a screening for the French distributors last night. We started back down the beach. The driver met us halfway and Francis had to hurry ahead to answer the radiophone in the car. One of the editors had some questions about the changes for tonight's screening.

When we got to the house we washed the mussels and the clams and steamed them. We ate them dipped in melted butter. I thought the mussels were great, really tender and flavorful. Francis is still at the table with Walter, Carroll Ballard and Matthew Robbins. They are talking about the ending.

Trying to get a fix on it. As if, when they try to pin it down into something concrete, it slips away, goes out of focus. Francis is talking about the themes of the film. "We do things that contradict the way we define ourselves."

I can see that statement etched in the air. That's one of the elements that sent Francis into a tailspin of depression these past months.

April 3, Napa

Last night I saw a screening of perhaps two-thirds of *Apocalypse Now*. I was amazed at how, having been there, having seen most of the footage at one time or another, the assembled film was something other than I could have imagined. It had a life, a unique quality that was other than the sum of its parts. The French plantation scene and a big section of the ending were missing, but still, the life of the illusion was amazing to me.

250

Driving out here today, we talked about the discrepancy
between the experience of being out there making the film,
and what you see on the screen. The film doesn't convey
the heat, the concussion of the explosions, the excitement
of the helicopters, or shooting at 4:00 A.M. Being there,
your eye and experience took in so much more than the
camera. In the screening room, the film seemed more like
a memory or a dream.

I do think Francis's film is a real step toward film as
literature. Trying to include what Willard is experiencing
inside as well as out.

April 4, Napa

Last night we watched the Academy Awards. I was sad
because Francis wasn't with us. We have no television reception out here, so I went with the kids to Margie's parents' house. Margie's mother was the maid for the family
who originally owned our house. She lived on our property
for thirty-eight years. The family has a jolly warmth—they
spoke to each other in Spanish. Their three sons were there
and Margie's husband, their two boys and my three kids. I
sat on the floor in front of the TV and leaned against the
coffee table. Sofia made a nest of throw pillows and curled
up beside me. The coffee table was octagonal, wood, covered neatly with clear plastic. Margie's mother seemed concerned that I was sitting on the floor.

We all got to watching the TV in spite of the snowy
reception. Roman jumped up and down every time we
could see Marcia and George Lucas. He yelled and leaped

in the air and got everyone laughing when *Star Wars* won something. I was excited that Marcia won the editing award. Francis said today, "Since George didn't win any of the major awards himself, he'll be back. He won't just retire into moguldom as he's been saying. He'll come back, he'll make another film, he likes to win."

When Jane Powell came out to sing, the kids said, "Who's that?" She was Francis's teenage love; mine, too. I've been dying to see *Seven Brides for Seven Brothers* again. While she was on, the kids got up and jumped around. One of the boys got a baby chicken from the garage. It ran around flapping and peeping under the furniture, with Sofia chasing it. No one paid attention to the TV again until Farrah Fawcett came on.

I was happy to see Diane Keaton win. I remember she used to come to the *Godfather* set, very effervescent, in big boots, kooky clothes, and go into wardrobe and come out all flattened and straightened into Kay Corleone.

April 5, Napa

I stayed inside today. I have a lousy cold. I cleaned my office, opened a mountain of stale mail. I put bills in envelopes for the accountant, mailed in the card for Sofia's Brownie camp, filed paint chips and snapshots. I made out a check for a deposit on a summer tour of art and textile workshops in Japan. It was a strange feeling. It is the first time in fifteen years I have initiated a trip apart from Francis and the kids. I have taken little excursions for a few days once in a while, but all the rest of my traveling has been in relation to Francis or the children. I have fit things I wanted to see and do around their plans.

About four in the afternoon, Gio called. He missed the bus and asked me to pick him up. I walked outside. There seemed to be paintings everywhere. Shapes of light on white iris blossoms, patterns of petals on the paths by the cherry trees. Tulips leaning over, open wide, twisting and falling apart. Crisp ice poppies. There were new purple iris, all backlit, that must have just opened. They looked like ones on those Japanese screens. I thought about how it would look to stand a gold leaf panel behind them in the dirt of the garden. Then I remembered that I was on the way to the car and Gio.

April 6, Napa

This morning Francis and I were arguing in the driveway of the San Francisco house. The kids were already in the car waiting to go back to school in Napa. Finally, I went around to the driver's side. We continued shouting over the top of the car. It was cold and the windows were rolled up. The kids were inside, squirming around, throwing a cloth ball at each other. Sofia looked out at us arguing and yelled real loud, "Cut!" Francis started laughing. We both saw it at about the same moment. It was a terrific scene for a movie. Francis said, "Don't you think I wonder if I am just making my next movie right now? All this we're going through is just part of some movie. People tell me that during *Godfather* I was having spaghetti dinners with lots of wine and people around the table, and now I am this weird guy looking at my life, just like Willard. Don't you think it scares me that my life is just a movie I'm making?"

April 8, Napa

This morning I asked Francis what his inner voices were telling him to do. He said they tell him to do nothing, don't push, don't act, just wait. The complete opposite of the way he is used to being. He said he was afraid that his voices were telling him to be alone, with no one in his life. He said, "Can't you see how scared I am, Ellie? You are saying, 'Hurry up and define our marriage, I'm not waiting much more.' United Artists is saying, 'Hurry up and finish the film, we can't hold off the banks and exhibitors much longer,' and part of me is saying, 'Just tough it out, don't make some quick resolution in order to get off the hook.' " He said the more he works on the ending, the more it seems to elude him, as if it is there, just out of view, mocking him. He said, "Working on the ending is like trying to crawl up glass by your fingernails."

April 9, Napa

Saturday afternoon I wanted life to freeze-frame a moment. It was a perfect spring day. Fresh and warm. The garden was many shades of the most intense green. The flowers were just dots overwhelmed by the spectrum from shiny dark green/black to bright, translucent yellow/green. Francis seemed to be relaxed for a moment. He was on the lawn with Roman's seventh-grade class. They were making a movie called *Revenge of the Killer Grapes*. There were eight or nine girls dressed as grapes in green tights and puffy purple costumes stuffed with newspaper. Roman was the winemaker they were sneaking up on. Francis was helping the student director set up a shot. Gio and I were watching from the porch. Gio said, "You know, Mom, we could costume everybody in St. Helena. We have fifteen hundred pairs of Vietnamese pajamas in the barn."

George Lucas came over. The kids rushed him for autographs. When the shooting was finished, the teacher took the first load of girls home. When she went out to the highway, the boys went to the barn and got a dummy of a dead Vietnamese from the props storage and laid it in the driveway. When the teacher returned, they did a whole routine, firing a machine gun and exploding some balloons filled with fake blood.

Michael Herr, who wrote *Dispatches*, was here. He said it shook him up to see the bloody body lying there. That in Vietnam they'd have said, "Police up that gook."

I haven't taken any photographs for a long time. Francis gave me a little snapshot camera last Christmas with a built-in flash. I haven't felt like using it. Today I tried it out. I took some pictures of him on the porch, lying on the wicker couch. This evening I took some shots of Sofia play-

255

ing old maid with Francis, George Lucas and Michael Herr at the dining room table.

April 10, Napa

This afternoon I took a long walk, several miles along the dirt roads, toward the winery. There were wild sweet peas and lupine by the side of the road. I walked over by the helicopter pad. It hasn't been used for many months. There was a newly planted hill of vineyard behind it. Each new plant was protected by a Foremost ice-cream carton. The workers must have gotten them from the props in the barn. The last time I saw those cartons they were stacked up in a Medevac tent where I was sitting during the rain in Iba.

Several sea van containers were sent back from the Philippines when the production closed down. There must have been a general order to pack up everything and ship it. It was unloaded in the barn here. Some of it was used for shooting pickup shots last summer. There is a huge mound of dummies, there are fake army weapons, helmets, canteens, editing tables, period Coca-Cola cans, fans, Ifugao spears, totem poles, boxes of moldy books from the French plantation set, peanut butter, instant coffee, sheets, throw pillows, two Japanese bathtubs, GI uniforms, baseball mitts, grenade belts, C rations, Ifugao loincloths, baskets, fake jewelry, light fixtures, megaphones, office furniture, reference materials, Vietnamese sandals. The kids have Colonel Kilgore's surfboard in the swimming pool.

256

April 13, Napa

It was Francis's birthday Friday. Number three during the making of *Apocalypse*. There was a party at his office. He came here afterward. His gifts were unloaded onto the table in the hall. This morning I was straightening up. I couldn't help reading some of the cards. "Thanks for letting me participate in your greatness. Love . . ."

Some days I am tired and just want out. It seems hopeless. There will always be a fresh crop of adoring young protégées waiting in the wings. This current situation started during *Godfather II*. I was on location with Francis, away from San Francisco, my friends and the things that stimulated and interested me at the time. I was so angry with myself, angry that I couldn't just get totally happy focusing on Francis and the making of his film. Someone else did.

April 14, Napa

Francis was lying on the couch. He said, "Maybe the teeth of my soul have cavities."

April 15, Napa

I am aching today because I have asked Francis not to come out this weekend. I jump every time the phone rings. It just rang. A kid wanted to know if I'd drive Roman and him to the motorcycle shop. Then, a collect call from Gio asking if he could buy a dog in San Francisco. Some part of me expects Francis to call back. We had a long conversation last night and another one this morning. I was in a hysterical rage. I had inadvertently found out that Francis's other woman was with him for a screening of the complete film. I haven't been invited yet. I felt completely betrayed. In my mind's eye I saw a calendar, two years of days, flipping over real fast like in those old movies. There was a picture of something on each page, a photo of us riding to the set in a bonca, the insects around the lights on a rainy night, the boys at the airport, the dinner table on the two hundredth day of shooting, on and on.

Every part of me aches. I don't want to see Francis for a while. I don't know if I am helping him or escalating his dilemma, aiming for health between us or being weak. I don't know if I'm helping myself or cutting off the new buds of growth between us.

The phone rang. It was Francis calling on the radiophone in the car. He is on his way here.

April 19, Napa

Last Sunday, Francis and I had a giant Italian/Irish blow-out. It's as if the old stuff between us can't just fade away, it has to explode, be blasted out with dynamite. All Sunday afternoon I escalated the argument as if there were something I needed to vomit and couldn't. Finally, in the early evening, Francis grabbed up the stuff on the coffee table and threw it through the glass top. There was a stew of broken glass, candlesticks, nut bowl, Japanese teapot, cups, and tea-wet papers on the floor. I thought about how all of this is affecting the children. Sofia came into the living room; I guessed she should see what is true in our lives. She looked at the new table with its dented frame and broken glass. She said, "Oh, now you won't care if I put my feet up."

Monday my whole body ached as if I had taken some physical pummeling. Francis and I talked on the phone a long time, trying to understand why we have been blowing up our marriage chunk by chunk over the past year. In the afternoon I took a long hot bath. I called up a friend and drove into the city to have dinner and go to a movie. We went to see *An Unmarried Woman*. It seemed so clean and simple. The man cries, tells his wife he is in love with another woman and is moving in with her. The woman walks away and vomits and begins the process of going about her life. The husband in the movie comes back and says, "Can't you just consider that I was sick for a while?" That's what I have been telling myself for over a year now. Francis is not well.

Yesterday I went to the post office. A new girl from Sofia's class was playing outside. I had heard that she recently moved here to live with her grandmother. I asked if she could come home with me to play with Sofia for a while. On the one-mile ride to our house she told me that her mother died on February 13. She said their car was caught in a mud slide during a storm, but she didn't die from that, she only got a cut on her forehead. She died from pneumonia afterward. She said she almost died in the car herself, but she got out the hatchback. She said her twin sister died at the age of five weeks from a heart attack at 5:00 A.M., on October 9, her mother's birthday. She said her grandmother wouldn't believe it until she saw the notice in the newspaper. She said her cat died. When she saw our big Victorian house her eyes filled with tears. She said, "Do you have twisty stairs?" I said, "Yes." She said, "That's scary." We had arrived at the back door. She jumped out of the car and ran across the lawn to swing with Sofia. I was startled by the way she sort of reported the events of her life. There was no possible way to integrate them into her six years of living.

April 20, Napa

Apocalypse Now is still going on. There is a huge editing staff. There are screenings. There are people shooting inserts and recording narration. A huge sound and music department is gearing up. Schedules are being made and revised, there are opticals and lab work to do. There is a sign-up sheet for a company roller skating party and wine is served some evenings. A singing telegram from Kurtz arrived to keep up lagging spirits. A big production continues, but it is in my peripheral vision.

Today the children are in school, I shut off the telephone. I am completely alone. I love it.

April 22, Napa

Yesterday, I drove to the city. The air was clear and the hills looked very close, they were fuzzy with thick grasses and patches of wild flowers. The places where there were cows looked like postcards of Switzerland. Cows, standing in a sea of green, sprinkled with buttercups and lupine. I went to a screening of some footage from the documentary. I haven't looked at any of it for a year. I was pleased that it looked okay.

It was strange to look at what seems like a former lifetime. I was in a couple of clips myself. I looked younger with short hair. A different person. Francis was someone else, too. There was a shot with him standing by Gio. He was fifty pounds heavier and Gio was a little kid. Now Gio has a mustache and hairy legs.

April 23, San Francisco

I am in an editing room. It is semidark. They are changing reels on the KEM. Three rolls of sound track and one picture track are being threaded onto sprockets around heads to the take-up cores. Bright yellow strips of leader are snaking through the machine. A patch of wall behind is rust color. Everything else is in silhouette from the one small work light. We have just seen several reels of a new cut of the ending. I am feeling this rush of emotions. It seems out of place. Everyone else is chatting.

It is Sunday. The crew is working, getting ready for the first big screening. In two days, nine hundred people will come at 9:30 in the morning to see this cut. Francis will be reading their reaction. He says he is really scared. He is.

Recently he said he realized that when he came back from the Philippines he had wiped out the base of his financial security, and when he looked at all the footage, he didn't know if he was a fool or an artist. His personal life was in conflict. There was no safe part of his life to hold on to, so he crashed.

April 25, San Francisco

I am waiting. Francis is meeting with the publicists. There is a stack of response sheets from this morning's screening on the coffee table. Francis is dividing them into two piles, ones that liked the film and ones that didn't. They are talking about how strongly the audience reacted. Francis is saying, "It's not working the way I want it to. I am trying to figure out the next steps."

The question is whether or not to show the whole film to the exhibitors for bidding and play dates, or show only parts of it.

April 28, San Francisco

I am in Francis's office. He has forty-eight file cards in a long, uneven line on the floor. Each card has a different scene typed on it. He is moving them around to restructure the film.

April 30, San Francisco

I am in Walter's editing room. We just saw a new cut of the opening of the film. I had a wave of sheer terror. Parts of my body are still rippling with electricity. This opening is not as good as the previous one. It is trying something else and doesn't make it yet. The last cut is all apart and can't be reassembled. The screening for the exhibitors is in two days. Francis just said, "If they don't like the film, and don't bid on it, we won't have to come out with it." There is nervous laughter.

It is Sunday. I wonder where the editors' families are. Our kids are in Napa. Roman was weeping when we left. He said he didn't have anyone to play with, didn't have anything to do. I felt bad most of the way to San Francisco, feeling that I should have stayed with Roman, feeling Francis was in a hurry, not wanting to keep the editors waiting, knowing Roman has to learn to meet his own problems without Mom to help, but filled with guilt that I am not there enough for him. Roman is the most like Francis. When Francis has been troubled, I think Roman has felt it the most.

Now the editing machine is stopped on a frame of Willard lying on the hotel bed. There is editing clutter all around me. Rolls of tape, splicers, white mitts, Dust Off, cores, reels, schedules, rubber bands, coffee cups, rewinds, notebooks and racks and racks of thin boxes with a roll of sound or picture. Each box has a numbered yellow-tape spine. I wonder what is in box RK4012–4710 or BD7012–7814. Several work lights illuminate sections of the room. There are no windows, I can't see time changing. Maybe it is 4:00 P.M., maybe it is 4:00 A.M. Francis is out at the typewriter rewriting a section of narration to try over this cut. I am hungry.

May 2, Napa

Francis just called. He was on his way to the exhibitors' screening. He said that taking the film apart and trying to make major changes in this short time wasn't practical, wasn't intelligent, but somehow it was right. The evolution of the film is continuing. The screening just came at the wrong time. He described what he had done. How he had restructured the beginning. Now, Willard was in the hotel room, waiting to be debriefed and going back over the experience, rather than in the hotel room waiting for a mission. Essentially, he is trying to use the hotel room as bookends. Starting there and ending there rather than ending with Kurtz Compound exploding as the last scene.

May 10, Flight from New York City to San Francisco

The stewardess has just told us that the duck on the menu has been changed to chicken. Francis and I are on a flight back to San Francisco. The past six days we spent in New York are now many memory fragments.

Francis had a screening for the exhibitors. He didn't show the whole film. He decided that it will not be possible to finish the film for a December release and will have to postpone the opening until spring of 1979.

I found this note in the typewriter that he had written to himself:

What are my problems?

My greatest fear—I've had for months— The movie is a mess— A mess of continuity, of style—and most important, the ending neither works on an audience or philosophical level. Brando is a disappointment to audiences—the film reaches its highest level during the fucking helicopter battle.

My nerves are shot— My heart is broken— My imagination is dead. I have no self-reliance— But like a child just want someone to rescue me . . ."

The same day I found this item in the gossip column of a New York paper:

Lightning strike twice? Will Francis Ford Coppola pull off his fantastic success of The Godfather movies a second time, with his way-over-budget, terribly expensive but highly touted "Apocalypse Now"?

The recent exhibitors' screenings for it on both coasts had people clawing to get in, and a tighter security than any in past history. Those who made it left after in a state of shock, muttering, "It's staggering." One person commented, "There has never been a film to compare it to," and another said, "Monumental. It will create a new level of movie standards."

———

We had lunch with Bernardo Bertolucci. He looked like Francis, dark around the eyes, his vibrant energy drained away. The last time I saw him was a few years ago. It was a warm night, we were walking through the streets of Rome. Bernardo was telling jokes and Francis was singing, wearing Bernardo's hat.

Bernardo talked about how, after *Last Tango*, he felt a kind of omnipotence. Then during *1900* he fell into a depression and hypochondria that stopped the shooting several times. He said his next film would be small. It was about a woman and child. He would work on themes from his own childhood with his mother, almost like a kind of therapy. He talked about Italy and the political situation, about his difficulty in finding a background setting for his film that depicted Italy today and wasn't kidnappings and fire bombings. He talked about how the kidnapping situation had gotten so out of hand, partly because the political parties in Italy used the issue to blame each other for how bad things were. He said that in France, where the government had dealt very harshly, it was not the same problem.

We went to the Metropolitan Museum. The Monet show has already closed. I looked at Chinese ceramics. Francis was bored. He stood back watching the people until we came to an exhibit from the reign of Napoleon, which interested him. At closing time we were ushered out through the Egyptian section. I loved the wall paintings, the coral and terra-cotta colors with blue, green and gold details. In the evening we had dinner with Nan and Gay Talese. We went to Elaine's. I hadn't been there for about three years. It was like you read about. Bernardo was at the next table, Bob Fosse and one of his dancers at the next. Woody Allen was seated by himself, like a caricature of a lonely little man. Bob Fosse didn't look well. Francis and Bernardo had shadows of some personal lingering depression. Woody Allen looked miserable. I hear Marty Scorsese is not well. What is happening to all these directors?

Nan and I talked. She said her husband had been writing his book about sexuality in America for the past six years. She said that was what her ten-year-old daughter's entire conscious memory was of her father's work. I said that was true about Sofia, too. She was four when Francis started *Apocalypse Now*. She is going to be seven next week. She thinks that is what Daddy does.

One afternoon I went to Soho and met my old boyfriend. I hadn't seen him for perhaps a dozen years. He is a painter. He took me to his gallery and pulled out some paintings from the storage racks in back. The room seemed familiar. I realized it was the gallery location used in the film *Unmarried Woman*.

Something inside me started to laugh. I was standing in

the exact fantasy of my girlhood. There I was in a big gallery with this artist, an intellectual cowboy with a sense of humor, showing me his paintings. Telling me about them. Other people were crowding around.

He took me to lunch. We talked. He remembered all sorts of little details about things we had done together. I don't have that kind of memory. Francis does. As he talked, I realized that he is the same kind of romantic as Francis, with the same kind of obsession about his work, same vivid, visual fantasy life. A person easily bored, continually setting impossible goals, stimulated by risks and crises.

He talked about his personal life. He said after six years of therapy he had decided to give up trying to fit the reality of family life together with his romantic illusions and he had opted for romance. His children spent part of the time with him and part of the time with his wife in California.

There was a dot of green paint on his left ear.

May 11, Napa

We hiked up to the dam and across the hills and down to the meadow at the foot of the olive grove. The army tents that were set up for last summer's shoot are still there. There is a totem pole with horns, carved heads and a fire pit at its base. It was used for some pickup shots of Willard as a captive at Kurtz Compound.

Some people on horseback who rode through our property a few weeks ago reported to the sheriff that we had a Manson-type group living here.

May 12, Napa

Lately Francis has been talking about his fears. His fear that he can't write an ending for his film. His fear that he can't write. That his greatest success has come from adapting someone else's writing. My guess is that when he gives up, when he concludes he is not the kind of novelist or playwright he dreamed of being as a young boy, he will know what kind of a writer he is and it will be more right for him than anything he could have imagined.

June 8, Napa

I went to have lunch with Marcia Lucas at her house. We sat outside in the patio. Marcia had planted the flower beds and laid all the brick herself. George came down from his writing room in his slippers and T-shirt and ate with us. I asked Marcia if she would edit my documentary. She said she was putting her house in order. She had worked so hard for so many years without stopping she wanted to stay home for a while. She advised me to edit the film myself. I could hear myself saying, "But I wouldn't know where to begin." She said I could just start with an assistant and learn how to do it.

June 9, Napa

For the last two weeks Francis has been reading the Mishima books starting with *Spring Snow*. He is on the third one in the quartet now. This morning we sat on the porch talking about Japan. We talked about how Tokyo has a kind of energy, perhaps from Western technology colliding with Eastern tradition. Europe seems romantic and connected to the past, almost out of date. The United States has technology without much soul. India is spiritually developed but can't feed its people. Japan seems like the one place where the material and the spiritual world, the yin and yang, the left and right side of the brain, the masculine and feminine are coming together.

Francis has been talking about setting his next film in Japan. He said there has never been a successful American film set there. "Hollywood thinks people don't want to see films set in Japan." I remember when he started on *Godfather II*, people said, "What are you doing that for? There's never been a sequel that was any good."

As Francis talked about the next film he wanted to make, I felt myself getting high just thinking about it. He was not seeing the film completely, but more intuitively, knowing it was there and would come into focus.

By the time he left for the office, we had talked about what if he just went to Japan and got a small apartment in Tokyo, took language lessons, cooking and kendo lessons and wrote a journal. A whole romantic vision took shape. It felt like the beginning of the next episode of our lives. The outlines of the next film fading in.

June 11, Napa

It is Francis's father's birthday. The house is full of people. I can hear Francis's sister Tally practicing the cello on the front porch. She is preparing for a part in John Frankenheimer's next film. John and his wife are here. They are still asleep. John cooked dinner last night. He brought containers of stock from Los Angeles and his special boning knife. He made a great chicken dish. We opened a bottle of 1890 wine from the old Inglenook cellar.

I am looking out the window where I have watched the leaves fall, watched them be raked away. I have watched the light change the pattern of shadows on the lawn. Now I can see Francis's mother playing with Sofia and Tally's child, Matthew. The children are running around the lawn, falling down and rolling over in the grass while she pretends to catch and tickle them. Francis is over by the pool talking to Richard Brautigan's wife. She is a beautiful young Japanese woman. They are drinking from some square wooden cups she brought. I can tell Francis is fascinated.

July 5, Napa

Saturday, Francis and I started talking; we talked all day and evening until 4:00 A.M., when we fell asleep. We got up

Sunday and began a conversation that lasted until Monday morning at 5:00 A.M. Monday we got up about noon. I realized that Sofia's hair hadn't been brushed for two days. Ester cooked Sunday dinner and we sat down with the kids together. I don't know what else they ate during that time. I don't know what they were doing. They were here.

As we talked, I traveled through every emotion. I laughed, I was enraged, I was bored, I cried, I witnessed. I was the mother forgiving her son for his sins, I was the angry wife, I was the kindly therapist encouraging him to go on.

At the time, I could feel the different emotions coursing through my body, my mind. I tried to just observe them. Monday I tended to things about the house and the children. Tuesday, as I got out of bed, I started to cry, my body shaking, then laughing and crying again. It was a perfectly formless letting go.

Francis kept coming up to the bedroom. He wanted me to get up and come downstairs. He said I'd feel better if I'd get up. Guests were arriving for the Fourth of July. We were having a party.

I didn't feel okay until nearly three in the afternoon. When I went downstairs, people seemed glad to see me. Nobody asked where I'd been.

July 10, Napa

Barlow once told me, "Ellie, if you want to understand Francis, if you want to understand your relationship, God, just look at his movies." Perhaps I am up so close they are a blur.

272

All these months I have been talking about the themes of the film, talking about the innate contradictions in "man" while, in every way, I have been trying to disprove and rationalize the contradictions in my own life. It has taken until now for me to accept that the man I love, my husband, the father of my children, the visionary artist, the affectionate family man, the passionate and tender lover, also can lie, betray and be cruel to people he loves.

July 13, Napa

I am in my office with its newly painted bright yellow walls. I have pinned up a jumble of Sofia's drawings, Japanese prints, postcards, stamps, labels, a valentine, a piece of African fabric that is electric blue with orange, green, red and black geometric designs. Out my window is a summer afternoon. Dry and hot. Now the small green grapes are in clusters hanging under arms of thick leaves.

Roman has gone to France to spend the summer with a French family. Gio is in Canada working on his first job. Francis is in San Francisco. Sofia is rehearsing in a children's theater production of *The Wizard of Oz*. She is a Munchkin. I am preparing to go to Japan. The family won't be all together again until September.

September 14, Napa

Sofia is running into my room and back out to the mirror. She is trying on a kimono, a field jacket and a piece of handwoven fabric I brought back from Japan. The suitcase is open on the floor of my bedroom. It is a jumble of wrinkled clothes wrapped around some ceramic pieces, rolls of kimono cloth, packages of handmade paper. Now Sofia has a piece of fabric tied around her like an Ifugao loincloth. She is trying to remember the steps of an Ifugao dance she learned. Roman has put on an old blue and white men's kimono that I bought in a flea market in Kyoto. He has tied the belt real low and is stuffing a pillow in the front trying to look like a sumo wrestler.

I came home yesterday. Francis, Roman and Sofia met me at the airport. On our way back to Napa we drove by Gio's new boarding school. He looked inches taller, tan and self-confident with kind of a surfer cool, wearing a secondhand-store Hawaiian shirt. In his room he had a Japanese bed on the floor, some photos and posters and a little refrigerator. His roommate had a desk and a bunk bed and name labels in his clothes.

Francis said that when Roman got off the plane from France he was wearing knee shorts and a beret. He had a long loaf of French bread under his arm and a bottle of wine.

September 30, Napa

Francis is a master of creating illusion. He is one of the most skilled professionals in the field around the world. Over and over again he creates the most convincing illusion that he sincerely wants to have a marriage and family life without a triangle. A little time passes and it becomes clear that it was an illusion.

I wonder if I will ever get to the point where I can see through the illusion while he is creating it. Maybe I am trying to break his natural gifts, his talents.

Today the I Ching said: "Deception and dishonesty in the emotions of a relationship, even if tacitly agreed to by both people, keep the relationship from becoming a close one of love and unselfish passion."

October 2, Napa

I heard the French plantation scene is definitely out of the picture. It never seemed to fit right. I am one of the people who liked it, but it did stop the flow of Willard's journey. Today I was thinking about all the days of agony Francis went through during the shooting of that scene. The hundreds of thousands of dollars spent on the set and the cast flown in from France. Now the whole thing will end up as a roll of celluloid in a vault somewhere.

October 9, Napa

I asked the I Ching some questions lately. Twice I have gotten number 37, "The Family": "The family shows the laws operative within the household that, transferred to outside life, keep the state and the world in order . . . when the family is in order, all the social relationships of mankind will be in order."

October 12, Napa

All this year I have been asking Francis to set his limits and let me know what they are, as if then I would see if I could accommodate them. I set no limits, as if it weren't my prerogative. As if it were part of a marriage contract that you accept your husband's life-style, the location of his employment, his income and all the emotional givens as well. I resisted the parts I didn't like, but I never set any limits. This week I did.

October 18, Napa

Michael Herr, Francis and I were sitting at the breakfast table looking through the morning mail. Francis said, "I wish magazines would publish when they really had something to say." Michael said, "If *Newsweek* would search their heart, they'd probably come out twice a year."

October 19, Napa

Francis seems to be working on the film more, putting more of his attention there. He has locked the first half of the film and set the music cues. He is beginning to work with the musicians. He has started looping the actors' voices. He still has the editors working on the second half of the film. The ending is not finished. He is thinking of shooting one last scene.

October 25, Napa

Today I have a hangover. Maybe I am mostly tired. I slept about an hour and a half last night. Francis, Gio and I went to a Grateful Dead concert. Bill Graham invited us to watch from the stage. The road manager sat us on some trunks in the shadows about six feet from the drummer. He got us beer and Perrier from an ice chest under a section of the stage. The music was amazing. It had physical impact. I could feel it and hear it, but mostly I was watching the whole performance. A Hell's Angel was seated on a box about three feet from me. His left arm seemed to be inside his jacket like it had been wiped out in an accident. He took the glove off his right hand with his teeth. He had elaborate silver rings on three fingers. He wore jeans, a leather jacket that said Hell's Angels California on the back and heavy boots that laced up high under his pant legs. He had on a bandanna headband, dark glasses and a red silk scarf around his neck like the Red Baron. He had a leather bag that he opened, holding it between his feet and using his right hand. He took out a plastic bag with what looked like chewing tobacco and put a wad in his mouth. He opened another section of the bag and took out several tambourines and a rhythm instrument to shake, made out of metal and wood. He played the tambourine softly, hitting it against his boot, stopping occasionally to smoke or drink some beer. I could see another Hell's Angel in the shadows a few feet away. He had a reddish beard with a lot of gray in it. I was surprised to realize that these men were in their late thirties or early forties, Francis's age.

The lights kept changing and different things would come in and out of view. The road manager was sanding new drumsticks as he took them out of their plastic wrappers. He reached in and retrieved a stick that fell by the drummer's foot. He refilled his Perrier cup. He shifted people so he could get into equipment trunks.

There was a little kid, about eight, running in and out of the darkness. He had a Nikon camera on a strap around his neck. I heard someone ask him to please go out and get him a joint.

At the end of the set, we went back to the dressing room and Bill introduced us to Jerry Garcia. He reminded me of Francis, sort of portly with traces of gray in his black beard. He appeared to be a thoughtful, middle-aged man in the music business.

I met a friend in the hallway and was talking until I heard the music begin again. I went back to stage left and found that we had been moved to another position. I could see a different angle of the stage. It included the upper half of the guitarist and musicians in front. Someone said the Hell's Angel with the bad arm had a bullet lodged in his body that had never been removed. Slides taken during the Grateful Dead tour in Egypt were being projected on a huge screen above the musicians. There was a long sequence where just the two drummers played. The road manager opened the trunk we had originally been sitting on and passed out rhythm instruments to four or five people who seemed to be friends of the band. He moved a microphone to pick up their sound. At one point someone passed me a tambourine. I was too uptight to take it. I passed it to Francis. He shook it awhile and then I tried it. It was surprising how heavy it was and how tiring it got to keep up a rhythm. Bill Graham came by every little while. He said, "Look at the audience, look at that, the crowd isn't crazy, it's just weaving, everyone is joined together. It's a sociological phenomenon. Somebody ought to study it."

Something about the evening reminded me of the evening inside the Ifugao priest's house. It felt like the same thing. The scale was different, but everyone being joined together by rhythms and images was the same, and instead of rice wine and betel nut there was beer and grass.

At the end of the last set the band left the stage and the audience roared and clapped for an encore. Bill said to Francis, "Come on and see this. For fourteen years it has always been the same. They refuse to play an encore. I have to go back there and talk them into it. You want to see a performance? Come on and watch me." Francis went with Bill to the dressing room. About fifteen minutes later the band came back onstage for an encore.

We got home around three in the morning. We didn't go to sleep for a long time. We got up this morning at six. Francis had to catch a seven fifteen plane to Los Angeles and I had to take Gio back to school.

October 26, Napa

Last Saturday we had a huge harvest party. All the employees, the people working on the film, their families and friends; about three hundred people were invited to arrive at two in the afternoon and stay until midnight. During the morning, Francis and I were arguing in the bedroom. I guess the rest of the household could hear us and didn't want to interrupt, so when the truck arrived with the rented folding tables and chairs, napkins, wineglasses, etc., they were unloaded in front of the house instead of by the kitchen and the side lawn. When I looked out the window and realized what was happening, I went down and asked the gardener and Gio to help move things and set them up where they were supposed to be. I went back to the bedroom and Francis and I continued arguing. Several times during the week I had wanted to call the party off. It felt like last Christmas when we had this picturesque family affair with the Christmas tree we cut and decorated, the roast goose and chestnuts, garlands of greens on the mantels and fresh wreaths on the doors, ribbons and presents, eggnog and pumpkin pie. It looked so beautiful and felt so

280

terrible. Francis just lay on the couch, miserable and un-comfortable, dark circles under his eyes, totally joyless.

The guests started arriving right about two. At a quarter to three Gio came up to the bedroom and asked what to do. Weren't we coming down to the party? We showered and got dressed. Francis went down. I lay on the bed for a while with a cold washcloth on my face. My eyes were red and puffy from weeping. Finally I went downstairs at about three thirty. Hundreds of people had arrived. It was a perfect fall day, sunny and warm/cool with leaves floating to the ground. Grapes were being crushed in our new winery. Guests were watching and tasting last year's Cabernet Sauvignon. People were playing volleyball, Ping-Pong and bocce ball on the lawn. Children were in the pool, around the swing and playing with Gio's eight fuzzy black puppies. In the late afternoon a mariachi band began to play. They stood under the fig trees in front of the house. We had lots of Mexican beer, margaritas and a barrel of wine. Crepe paper streamers with paper flowers and piñatas decorated the wide veranda around the house. At dusk Mexican food was served by the wives of some of the workers. Homemade tamales, enchiladas and a side of beef that had been roasted in a pit and served with fresh chili sauce, beans, rice and tortillas. The long tables on the side lawn glowed with candles and fresh flowers from the garden. A Mexican flag flew from the flagpole.

All during the afternoon and evening people told me I looked radiant. They told me how happy they were to see Francis and me back together again. What a beautiful home and family we have. The band played all evening. The children asked for the Mexican hat dance over and over again. Everyone danced in the paved crescent in front of our handsome Victorian house. For a moment I walked out past the lights and sat on the lawn in the dark. I looked back. It looked like a beautiful movie.

October 29, Napa

Last night, when Francis and I went up to the bedroom, there was a fall chill. We lit the fireplace for the first time this season. We got into bed and watched the flames flickering and casting shadow shapes on the hearth and walls. Francis began talking about the ending of the film. It is still not clearly defined. Each time he looks at it, it seems to get a degree more in focus. This time we talked about the killing of the carabao scene. It's as if in the present cut, the killing of the carabao is sort of a dramatic backdrop for the killing of Kurtz. It is a powerful scene itself, a power statement. Francis was talking about bringing it into the foreground of focus, so its impact and meaning would not be diminished.

He talked about shooting one last scene where Willard tells Kurtz's son the wrap-up, the statement of what it is all about. Then he dropped that idea and began talking about opening the film with the theater dark and having jungle noises emerge out of the darkness before any images are seen on the screen. Then, if he didn't shoot another scene, ending the film with the boat on the river getting smaller and smaller, fading into darkness, and back to the sounds again before the houselights come on and the credits are rolled.

November 1, Napa

The leaves on the grapevines are turning burgundy red.
The trees near the house are a brilliant array of fall colors,
backlit and glowing in the afternoon sun. Sofia and a friend
are swinging double under the giant oak tree. Roman is
pushing them, and running to catch leaves floating down
like snowflakes in little gusts of warm wind. I am feeling a
moment of total calm, lying here on the lawn watching my
children and the season changing. The emotional extremes
of my life are at a little distance just now, although I know
they will return.

I realize I feel the highest highs being married to Francis
as with no other person I can imagine, and the bottom of
the pit of pits as well. I read a book recently called *Marriage
Dead or Alive* that pretty well sums up how I feel. It says:
"In marriage both partners confront each other with everything, with the healthy and the sick, the normal and the
abnormal traits of their essential being. The more one con-
fronts everything, the more interesting and fruitful it becomes. . . . Marriage is not comfortable and harmonious;
rather it is a place of inviduation where a person rubs up
against himself and against his partner, bumps up against
him in love and in rejection, and in this fashion learns to
know himself, the world, good and evil, the heights and the
depths."

November 3, San Francisco

I am on a PSA flight. Francis is sitting opposite me reading a script someone sent him. The light from the small, rounded, rectangular window is falling on his shoe, corduroy pant leg and a section of speckled carpet. His shoelace grommets look like sparkling pure gold. A few moments ago, Francis was saying that he had thought he would be always able to work. That he was not like an athlete, if he lost his legs he could direct from a wheelchair, if he lost his sight he could write with a Dictaphone. He said he never realized what he nearly lost—the only thing that counts: his mind.

We have been in Los Angeles, where Francis is looping at Goldwyn Studios. I went to meet him. As I drove up to the studio gate, there were signs that said, No Entry, No Parking, No Visitor Parking, No Parking for Casting Calls, No Parking for Extras. The guard was on the phone. He waved me to wait. There were five cars behind me by the time he came gruffly to my window. I said I was looking for Studio E where my husband Francis Coppola was working. His expression changed, he smiled and directed me to the right building and a parking space. When I found Francis he was sitting on a couch talking to a new young executive from United Artists who was asking about *Apocalypse Now*. Francis said he had set out to make a big, entertaining, action adventure film as a relief and change from all the heavy personal themes he struggled with on *Godfather II*. He said he thought in retrospect he could have made any film, a film about Mickey Mouse and it would have turned out the same. It would have become a personal journey into himself.

November 4, Napa

Yesterday I went with Francis to a screening of the last half
of the film to see some changes he was working on with the
editors. I hadn't seen any footage since June. There is no
question in my mind, beyond all my personal feelings and
connections, it is an extraordinary work.

It feels like Francis's level of desperation and fear is
shrinking. The lawyers and United Artists are starting to
talk more optimistically about the financial situation. There
is still more work to do in the final sequence at Kurtz Compound, but each cut seems to improve, get closer.

November 8, Napa

I have been reading one of the Oz books to Sofia. The
Patchwork Girl and her companions are traveling to the
Emerald City. They come upon an impassable high wall
with a gate that has a giant lock on it. They sadly conclude
they can go no farther. Then, a shaggy man tells them to
close their eyes and take one hundred steps forward. They
do, and when they open their eyes, they see that the gate is
far behind them. When they ask in amazement how it happened, the shaggy man says, "That wall is what is called an
optical illusion. It is quite real while you have your eyes
open, but if you are not looking at it the barrier doesn't
exist at all."

I find myself continually looking to see if this phase of
our lives is over. When it's past, I probably won't know it,
won't see it until later, in the distance behind me.

Cast of Characters

Francis Coppola	my husband, executive producer/director/writer of *Apocalypse Now*
Gio, Gian-Carlo Coppola	our older son (age 12 when production began)
Roman Coppola	our younger son (age 10)
Sofia Coppola	our daughter (age 4)

CAST OF CHARACTERS (in order of appearance)

Dean Tavoularis	production designer
Alex Tavoularis	sketch artist
Angelo Graham	art director
Bob, George R. Nelson	set decorator
John La Sandra	construction coordinator
Vittorio Storaro	director of photography
Enrico Umetelli	camera operator
Alfred Marchetti	key grip
Mauro Marchetti	2nd assistant cameraman
Mario Marchetti	2nd grip
Luciano Galli	gaffer
Gray Frederickson	coproducer

286

Fred Roos	coproducer
Doug Ryan	documentary assistant
Larry Carney	projectionist, documentary assistant
Marlon Brando	actor who portrays Colonel Kurtz
Harvey Keitel	actor
Francie, Frances Tavoularis	Alex Tavoularis's wife
Martin Sheen	actor who portrays Captain Willard
Jan, Janet Sheen	Martin Sheen's wife
Marc Coppola	production assistant, my nephew
Tonia, Antonia Storaro	Vittorio Storaro's wife
Francesca Storaro	daughter (age 9)
Fabrizio Storaro	son (age 7)
Giovanni Storaro	son (age 4)
Bobby, Robert Duvall	actor who portrays Colonel Kilgore
David Nowell	assistant aerial cameraman
A. D. Flowers	special effects coordinator
Josh, Joshua Weiner	photographer
Nat Boxer	boom man
Pete Kama	military adviser
Sue, Susan Arnold	baby-sitter and later assistant editor
Robin Ludwig	in charge of housekeeping
Mona Skager	associate producer
Dennis Hollis	transportation captain
Bill Graham	theatrical producer
Dick White	aerial coordinator/helicopter pilot
Joe, Joseph Lombardi	special effects coordinator
Bob, Robert Mondavi	owner Mondavi Winery
Mike, Michael Bernstein⎱ *Arlene Bernstein⎰*	friends and co-owners of Mt. Veeder Winery
Ester, Estrella Lambunao	housekeeper
Sam, Samuel Bottoms	actor who portrays Lance

Jerry Ziesmer	1st assistant director
Albert Hall	actor who portrays Chief
Eva Gardos	production assistant
Christian Marquand	actor in the French Sequence
Aurore Clement	actress in the French Sequence
Dennis Hopper	actor who portrays free-lance photographer
Mary Ellen Mark	photographer
Dennis Jakob	editor
Dennis Murphy	Marine coordinator
Bill, William Neil	my brother, documentary assistant
Jimmy, James Keane	actor
Fred, Frederick Forrest	actor who portrays Chef
Caterine Milinaire	writer, photographer
Pete Cooper	Marine coordinator (PBR)
Barry Malkin	editor
Tom Sternberg	production executive
Gary Fettis	set decorator's leadman
Doug Claybourne	assistant director
Jerry, Gerald Endler	special effects man
Delia Javier	set dresser
Walter Murch	picture and sound editor
Barlow Wetzell	a close friend
George Lucas	filmmaker
Steve, Steven Spielberg	filmmaker
Carroll Ballard	filmmaker
Carol Adrienne	a close friend
Matthew Robbins	filmmaker
Margie, Margarita Espinosa	housekeeper
Michael Herr	author
Bernardo Bertolucci	filmmaker
Nan Talese	book editor
Gay Talese	author
Jerry Garcia	musician, a founder of Grateful Dead